DEAR ME LET'S TALK

A DIALOGUE BETWEEN ME, MY SELF, & I AM

SHAWN ELLIOT RUSSELL

SER PUBLISHING

TEXAS

Copyright © 2016 by Shawn Elliot Russell

All rights reserved. To reproduce this book or any portion thereof, please contact the publisher to obtain written permission unless for the use of brief quotations in a book review. Thank you.

SER Publishing
7024 N. 17th St.
McAllen, TX. 78504
serpublishing@gmail.com
561-706-8043

Cover Design by: Shawn Elliot Russell

Dear Me, Let's Talk
A Dialogue Between Me, My Self, & I AM

Library of Congress Control Number: 2016908342

ISBN-13: 978-0-9972690-2-4 (Paperback)

10 9 8 7 6 5 4 3 2 1

1. Self Help 2. Mind Body 3. Spirituality

First Paperback Edition

Printed in U.S.A.

For My Mom, Pop, & Arlene

Thank you for being my support system, giving me the room to grow, and having faith in my journey.

I love you.

CONTENTS

ACKNOWLEDGEMENTS	I
INTRODUCTION	V

ME

1. Hopeless (Tired of Life)	1
2. I'm Broken (Happiness)	7
3. Taking Things Personally	17
4. I'm Not Special	25
5. Worry & Fear	33

MY SELF

6. Loneliness	43
7. Suffering	49
8. Trusting My Self	57
9. Letting Go (Control)	67

I AM

10. Who Am I? (My True Self)	79
11. What's the Purpose?	93
12. What is God?	101

AFTER THOUGHTS   119

"It takes love, nothing else. We can't **EVOL**ve without it, it's embedded in the word itself."

Acknowledgements

I have been very blessed in my life to be surrounded by people that allow me to find my way. At times, I can become secluded, distant, and irritable. As I continue this journey of stripping away old habits that don't serve me anymore, I work to wholeheartedly connect with myself and others in a compassionate way which requires me to be vulnerable. Vulnerability can be a scary thing when you've already taught yourself that it leads to pain, but still I try. This is me, retraining myself to accept vulnerability as a vital part of life; a part I was missing for a long time.

Mom and Pop, thank you for always supporting me. Throughout my creative endeavors, you've stood by my side and cheered me on. Your belief in me gave me the foundation I needed to feel comfortable trying. In 2006, when my world crumbled, you supported me and created a safe space to recover. Over the years, despite my attitude or distance, you stayed by me and worked to give me every opportunity possible. I thank you from the bottom of my heart. I love you.

Arlene, my angel, you have never left my side. Even when I was consumed with anger and bitterness, you stayed with me. When I felt I couldn't drive to work due to anxiety, you drove me. When I'd wake up in panic attacks, you'd let me hug you tight. When I felt like I was going crazy as I dove deeper and deeper into my mind, you listened with compassion and understanding. You have such a beautiful spirit. Thank you for being a great momma bear. I love you.

Lamar, my brotha from anotha motha. To me, you have always been a shining example of what a human being can be. Your kindness, understanding, and love for people has inspired me on many occasions. In times of turmoil, I have found myself asking, "What would Lamar do?" Thank you for your friendship and for our conversations over the years. Thank you for always encouraging me and pushing me when I needed that extra shove to get out of my comfort zone. "You either do it or you do it." I love you, brotha.

Father, thank you for always encouraging me to purse my dreams the best I can. You showed me how to take an idea and make it into reality. You demonstrated what it was like to really put your all into creating something. Remember the bright orange car stopper with the little red light at the top? Or the pants you sewed that allowed me to pull that rose out of nowhere? I still give my all in everything I do while paying attention to the details. Thank you for that foundation. I love you.

Anna, Rodney, Tres, & Mark, your friendship has meant the world to me. Anna, we may have lost touch over the years, but I always felt in my heart that we would pick up where we left off. I feel honored to be your friend. You have such a kind

ACKNOWLEDGEMENTS

heart and beautiful spirit. Thank you for being my ladybug. Rahdizzle, my dear friend, it's amazing to me that over 10 years ago you were telling me about some of the very things I found myself discovering recently. In every way, you truly are ahead of your time. Tres, we haven't known each other long, but it feels like a lifetime. Thank you for our late night conversations and your friendship, they hold a special place in my heart. Mark, your humor and friendship over the years has been a shining moment in my life. We may not speak often, but every time we do I love it. Thank you for always reaching out. I love y'all!

To everyone that took the time to read the drafts of this book, I greatly appreciate you. It means the world that you would put aside time in your day to read through this book. Nianna, thank you for offering your editing suggestions. I am now better versed in the use of "who", "whom", "then", and "than". You are awesome!

Introduction

The pages of this book contain my personal journal documenting the inner dialogue that took place between my Self and I over a 3 month period after years of intense anxiety and distress. I say my "Self", referring to a part of me I didn't know existed, because the answers I received concerning my tribulations offered a deeper wisdom than my thinking mind could imagine. In February of 2016, I began keeping a journal of these dialogues. I hoped it would help me find clarity during a time painted with fear, loss, confusion, and hopelessness. It turned out to far exceed my expectations. Allow me to share with you a little bit of my journey that led to the creation of this book.

It was August of 2013 when I found myself in the back of an ambulance on my way to the emergency room. After an increased heart rate, chest pains, and an impending feeling of doom came over me at work, the head nurse at the nursing home suggested the paramedics be called. Several hours later, I was informed that the results of the my EKG and blood tests came back normal. I was handed a prescription for Xanax and discharged. In the coming months, I'd fall deep into a cycle of panic attacks, fatigue, derealization, agoraphobia, gastritis, weight loss, and mental turmoil. It was a repeat of something that happened to me in 2006; something I thought had passed and would never return. Desperately seeking help, and unable to take medication to ease the constant anxiety due to the severe adverse reactions I would experience, I began searching for alternatives. One of those alternatives was mindfulness meditation. Initially, I felt it made me worse. The sensations of fear and derealization (a state in which you feel as if everything is a dream and you're not quite connected to yourself) would become heightened during and after the meditation. I'd later learn they weren't heightened, I'd only quieted down the mental noise that was keeping me from truly experiencing what my body and mind were going through. I vowed not to meditate again. Trying to regain some semblance of my life, I engaged in things I used to enjoy such as golf, ping pong, bike riding, making music, etc. It worked for a short time but, in August of 2014, I found myself back in the grips of fear. Out of options, I decided to try meditation again. I promised myself I'd push through any discomfort because, after all, what more did I have to lose? That promise turned out to be one of the best decisions of my life.

I often contemplated issues after meditating because I found I was able to understand them better when my mind and body were in a state of relaxation. However, only minutes later, I'd forget whatever understanding I came to. I began taking notes in my phone throughout the day as glimpses of insights about my situation, or something I was trying to wrap my head around, flashed in my mind. One day, after meditation, I closed my eyes and asked myself a question. Almost immediately, an answer popped in my head. I opened my eyes and grabbed my phone, typing as quickly and accurately as I could. There was no thought involved, just the typing of whatever words were streaming through my mind. Because I wasn't thinking, as the words appeared on the screen I had a chance to read them from a different perspective; as if they were not my own but those of someone else offering me insight. It felt like a conversation, and I found myself asking new questions as I sought clarification. Again, answers sprung forth and I typed furiously. This process continued until the questions and answers ceased. When it was all said and done (roughly 30 minutes later), I had a record of the internal dialogue I'd experienced many times. It wasn't until several months later that I realized I had enough written to create a book. After sending several chapters to family and friends for feedback, I received encouragement to pursue publishing them due to their personal yet universal nature. They felt others may benefit from their message and intimacy. As a result, I now humbly offer this book to you with the hope that you may find peace within its pages.

Due to my experiences these past three years, I've come to believe in a higher source that animates and guides everything in the universe. Sometimes I call it God, sometimes I call it Consciousness or Energy. I believe, in moments of stillness, we can feel its guidance and wisdom. I'm not sure where the answers that found their way into this book came from, but I like to think that for those brief moments I was connected to something greater. The answers contained within are my own personal understanding, I do not claim them to be universal truths or professional advice. I simply offer you my journal, chronicling a very difficult and special time in my life, as a way to let you know that you are not alone in your journey.

I think we all go through similar circumstances of varying degrees containing the emotions of fear, anger, sadness, joy, love, happiness, and everything in between. These circumstances can make us feel alone, as if no one in the world could possibly know what we're going through or help us overcome it. However, after observing that we all feel these emotions and, at times, share the same thoughts about ourselves and life, I can now see an amazing thread that ties us together: Our humanity. May this book help you feel less isolated by demonstrating that we have more in common than we often realize. You are not alone, we are here for you, and we understand. Thank you for taking the time to read *Dear Me: Let's Talk*, I hope it connects with you in some way.

Sincerely,

ME

1
HOPELESS
(TIRED OF LIFE)

Sometimes I feel hopeless and get tired of living. I get sick of the constant struggle. Everyday I have to struggle with something. My job, my never-ending worrisome thoughts, my health, something. It gets so tiring that sometimes I don't want to deal with it all anymore and I think about what it would be like to not be alive. Is that bad?

Do you think it's bad?

I think it means I'm depressed and something is wrong.

That something is wrong in general or that something's wrong because you occasionally have thoughts about not being alive?

I guess, because those thoughts pop in my head, I think something's wrong with me.

And how do you feel when those thoughts pop in your head?

Scared. I don't want to think like that. I don't know why I do. I feel like a part of me wants to die and a part of me wants to live, does that make sense?

Yes. I also think it's normal.

Really?

I think, if the average person were completely honest, they would admit to having occasional thoughts about what it would be like to not be alive anymore so they didn't have to deal with the stress of it.

Really?

I believe there are times when people may think about death bringing them peace.

Isn't that considered suicidal? Isn't that a problem?

They're just thoughts. Now, if you start planning it and really putting effort into how you're going to do it, perhaps you want to speak with someone. That means you've lost sight of the fact that what you're going through cannot break you and shall pass in some way, shape, or form. And, that's ok. You're not "bad" or "messed up" for that, you're simply in need of guidance. We think nothing of those who get lost without a map and need GPS to find their way. Yet, we place a stigma on those who get lost trying to navigate their minds without prior instruction on how to do so. The truth of the matter is, overwhelming feelings pass and the peace you seek can't be found in death because, as far as we know, you can't feel any human emotion when you cease to be human. However, if it's an occasional thought that causes you distress or passes through your mind at times of extreme stress or emotion, I think it's normal. We try to equate not being alive anymore with feeling peace because there's no more life "stuff" to deal with. It's just the mind spitting out ideas and stories because you've decided, consciously or subconsciously, that this moment is too much to handle and you want it to stop bothering you. So, the mind starts offering ideas about how that can be accomplished. With as many stories as we hear about people taking their own lives due to feeling overwhelmed or hopeless, it's no wonder the mind goes back in its vast database and brings up that scenario. But it's just a thought, nothing more. It sticks around and becomes distressing when you decide to chase it or label it as a problem.

So it's not bad?

It's whatever you think it is. In and of itself, it's just a thought with a logical reason for being there. If you're getting distressed over it, that means you find it disturbing and don't want to take that course of action anyway. And, if you can brush it off as a passing thought, it's nothing more than that. Furthermore, if you think neither one of those things are bad, then they aren't.

Life just gets hard sometimes. It gets difficult to find the joy in it.

That's normal too, especially in a culture that teaches us that joy is something external to attain rather than internal to experience. You're always chasing it and sometimes that chase feels useless, as if you'll never catch up. However, if you're admitting that you don't want to die, and thoughts about dying bother you, then on some level you must find joy in life. On some level, you know there's potential for happiness. Do you know why else you're finding little joy in life right now?

No, why?

Because you're not attending to the pain within you that's keeping you away from it. You're witnessing the symptoms of it – the occasional thoughts about not living – but haven't addressed the root cause. It's not that you don't want to live, it's that you don't want to feel the way you feel, which is part of the problem. You keep running away from something that is begging for your attention: Your tender heart. Connect with it and the rest will fall into place. It's ok to feel overwhelmed. It's ok to have thoughts about wanting immediate peace or what it would be like to not deal with your stress anymore. However, it's really counter productive and inaccurate to think that there's only one solution to your issues and that solution is death. You are made to experience life. The experiences within it are not meant to break you. They can't break you. Think of the stories you've heard regarding people locked in concentration camps or taken as prisoners of war and how they were still able to find peace in those horrendous conditions. They're human, just like you. They're made of the same stuff and hold the same potential as you do. Even in the face of terrible trauma, they found their inner peace. Do you know why?

Why?

Because it was there all along. You're born with it. It's right there for the taking and it starts with a choice to not suffer anymore. You've trained yourself to believe that you can't handle these things so your mind thinks of a way out. Sometimes, that way comes in the form of a daydream about death. But what you're capable of and what you've trained yourself to believe are two very different things. Drop the stories about what's going on and deal with the moment. Choose to not run away. Be open to what's happening right now and take it from there. Stop denying yourself the opportunity to work through it by ignoring your capability to do so. Be still, choose to face the emotions and sensations that arise. Refuse to make yourself suffer anymore by perpetuating stories that make everything worse, such as "I can't", "Why me?", "I never catch a break", or "This is never going to get better." Drop those stories, they're just opinions made of past experiences and imagination, not prediction and fact. "I wish I were dead so I didn't have to deal with this," is just another story. It's fiction, let it go. Pick a better story or no story at all. Accept the moment for what it is and move on. Once you start training yourself to do that, you'll notice those thoughts you worry about will fade away or cease to have power and the peace you were hoping to gain from outside experiences will begin to rise within you naturally.

I feel a little more energized and hopeful.

That's good. And, the amazing part is, you didn't have to do anything to get that energy and hope. You didn't have to achieve a promotion at work or buy a house. There was no praise from others or tub of ice cream, you simply realized your potential. It's further confirmation that it was inside of you the whole time.

I didn't realize that.

Now you do. And, now that you do, you can call upon it. It's the energy people rally up before a big game when you see them jumping around or becoming laser-focused. It's the energy that a good battle cry can stir up inside of you. It's there, ready to be utilized. Death doesn't bring you peace, realizing your own potential and strength does. It lets you know that you can handle any circumstance that comes your way. Peace isn't found in the lack of obstacles, it's found in the confidence of being able to handle them. It's found in acceptance. It's found in you.

2
I'M BROKEN
(HAPPINESS)

I feel like something's wrong with me, like I'm broken. Why do I keep feeling like that?

Out of compassion, you just want to be ok. You want to feel "normal" and like everything will be fine. So, you look for evidence that you're not normal as a way of trying to protect yourself.

How is that protecting myself?

If you find evidence that you're not normal, then you can take action to become normal again. The irony is that you're not protecting yourself, you're causing yourself more pain by never accepting who you are. It hurts when others reject us. Imagine how much it hurts when we reject ourselves.

Why do I do that?

Out of habit. Somewhere along the way you started to believe that you're broken and have been reinforcing that belief ever since. Even when you are consciously trying to enjoy your day, that old thought will pop up out of habit. It's natural. As humans, we tend to label everything. These labels can drive our behavior if we're not conscious of them. If you had a moment when you felt ill at ease about some aspect of yourself, you may have labeled it as "truth" and "painful", thus taking action to change that truth in order to avoid the pain. If someone said you were unattractive, you may have felt emotional pain as a result. To avoid that pain, you began trying to make yourself more attractive, effectively reinforcing THEIR opinion that you AREN'T attractive. Over time, that opinion becomes your label and eventually you accept it as truth because the thought automatically pops up whenever the subject of beauty comes around. We forget that it started as someone else's label. Our labels often aren't our own, they're the ones we grew up listening to. The next time one arises, ask yourself where it may have originated from. Whatever the case, you have the choice to accept it as opinion or truth. If you find yourself automatically getting upset when a label arises, it's because 1) in the past you've associated it with a bad feeling, and 2) that's your body saying it's not a helpful thought. Either way, it's a signal from your body and mind that it's time to let go of your label or choose a different one.

There's nothing wrong with me then?

Of course not, how can anything be wrong with us when we're not born as right or wrong? Without prejudice, Life creates us. We simply exist.

Existence is pure, like a tree, because it is what it's created to be – nothing more or less. A tree may shed its leaves during winter, or have a crooked trunk, but do we view it as broken when its branches stand bare? We see it as a whole, as a unique and beautiful creation. We see it as pure existence, a tree just being what it was created to be. We understand it's not supposed to look like the others, and any difference it displays is precisely what makes it beautiful. Yet, somehow we forget the beauty of uniqueness when it comes to humans, even though we're exactly like the tree: We too are pure existence created to just be what we are. Any labels you apply to yourself - such as "broken", "weird", or "wrong" - are your own opinions, or the learned opinions of others, and have no bearing on the fact that you're as pure as the tree. If the term "broken" implies that something is missing or not working, and we are consistently being what we're created to be, how can we ever be broken?

I'm not sure.

In addition, how can anything be wrong with us for being different, when life has purposefully created us as unique, not as humans meant to fit into a singular idea of "normal"?

I understand what you're saying. It makes sense. But, honestly, I still feel bad that I wasn't born the same way as someone who is considered "normal". Some people don't have to worry about their mind being anxious. Some people don't have to worry about not being attractive. Why was I created this way when this way is painful? I just want to be able to enjoy life like everyone else, is that so bad? I just want to feel normal.

I'm sorry you feel so much pain at this time. It's understandable to think that you were dealt a bad hand when you see other people apparently winning the pot. But you were created how you were created, nothing more. There was no malice or intent to cause you pain. Some trees are born with green leaves, some with yellow. Why do we accept them as they are and view them as beautifully unique but not ourselves?

I don't know.

Because we choose to, that's the only difference. We choose to see a tree as a tree. We choose to see a person as good or bad, right or wrong, normal or abnormal. You view others as a reference point for your own sense of normality. But, how is this possible when everyone's unique? Because everyone is different there can be no baseline for "normal". Therefore, your quest for it can never be fruitful because your treasure doesn't exist. As you attempt to fit into an imaginary ideal, you regretfully feel the pain of never doing so. You see John XYZ living how you want to live and cause yourself pain for not doing so.

But maybe a part of me wants to do what they do. Maybe I want to hop on a plane and travel. Doesn't that justify the pain I feel for not being able to do so like a normal person? Like millions of people are able to do?

It certainly explains the source of the pain. What's stopping you from flying?

I get horribly anxious, it's a miserable experience. I just want to be able to get on a plane and not feel intensely fearful. Plenty of people can do that. That's why I feel broken. I just want to live how other people live; without these painful experiences.

Let's step back and look at your statement "*I just want to be able to get on a plane.*" Is it possible that you're adding stress by condemning yourself for not being able to do something the way you believe you should?

What do you mean?

Can you get a plane, yes or no?

Yes, but it causes me a lot of anxiety.

You CAN get on the plane and you feel anxious when doing so. That's the reality of what's happening. Yet, a moment a go, you stated that you "*Just want to be able to get on a plane,*" as if you couldn't. The rest of that statement was, "*And not feel intensely fearful.*" Adding storylines about what it should or shouldn't be doesn't change the reality, it only creates friction. We have reality and we have the storylines judging reality. You already suffer when dealing with anxiety. The judgments about what you should be able to do cause extra suffering because they fight reality. You're piling pain on top of pain. Wouldn't it be more productive, and less painful, to cease the judgments and instead concentrate your efforts on accepting your reality? After all, these judgments only exist because you've created them. Being anxious is only being anxious, the moment itself comes without labels or opinions attached to it. You are literally spending energy to perpetuate storylines that make you feel bad. If you have a desire to fly then fly. A part of you wants to do it regardless of the anxiety. You've decided this would bring you happiness. So, not only are you denying yourself the opportunity for happiness by creating a story about yourself that makes you suffer but you're also judging yourself based on this entirely self-created idea of normal. Can you see how this all exists in "yourself"?

...Yes.

I think it's time to start working on acceptance.

It's hard to accept things that cause me pain.

Acceptance is our birthright. Every time you become aware of something, you naturally accept it. It isn't until you begin creating stories about it that acceptance goes out of the window. Imagine a world where you only feel anxiety as anxiety, just as you feel air as air. No judgments, it just is what it is and you move on, like seeing an ex you've gotten over walk past you in the street. Believe it or not, this IS how you experience your anxiety prior to the judgments you place upon it. Until you create the habit of accepting yourself as you are, these emotions may continue to rise. Emotions can bring with them stories of the same texture. Because they feel so familiar, the hard part may be to accept your thoughts about feeling broken as only opinions and letting them go. As you work towards accepting yourself, you'll find that you're already complete have everything you desire inside of you already.

What do you mean I have everything I desire inside of me already?

At its core, your desire to be "normal" is the desire for peace of mind and happiness. These are internal experiences, happening inside of your body, not outside of it. Therefore, they are inside of you already. Tell me, what are some things that you believe would bring you happiness?

Let me think...money, success, being attractive, a life without anxiety. Those are few things I can think of that would definitely bring me happiness.

And how do these things bring you happiness?

Because if I had them I would feel happier.

But where would you feel the sensation of happiness?

In my heart. My mind would be peaceful.

So these sensations happen inside of your body?

I suppose so.

And did the money hand you a pill to swallow, effectively placing happiness inside of you?

That's a silly question, of course not.

It's only silly because I'm restating the obvious: Money can't literally give us happiness. Yet, we say things like, "Money brings me happiness," because we mistakenly believe it's the money that's responsible for happiness arising within us. If money doesn't literally give us happiness, then where must it be in order to feel it "in your heart"?

Inside of me already, I suppose.

Exactly. We choose the things we believe will make us happy. When we attain them, we say to ourselves, "I'm happy now!" But do you see what evoked the happiness? Our declaration, nothing more! When we finally decide to be happy is when our body and mind say, "Ok!" and the energy of happiness rises within us.

So, if I tell myself to be happy right now I will be?

Only if you wholeheartedly believe it. If you

actually believe you're unhappy, unhappiness prevails. If you want to test this theory, think of a memory that "brings you happiness". Try to wrap yourself up in it: The way the air felt, the sounds, the physical sensations of wherever you may have been. Immerse yourself. What do you feel?

Happy! I thought of a time I was at the beach with my family and I began to feel happy.

See, you're not at the beach. Yet, you were able to evoke the feeling of happiness. It's always there inside of you. You only need the right conditions for it to arise. Same goes for love, courage, joy, gratitude, etc.

What conditions do I need?

Choosing to experience and connect with what's happening without judgment creates the condition for happiness to arise. Embracing the moment, instead of trying to deny or avoid it, opens the door for your innate spirit of exploration, creation, and connection to flourish, thus creating happiness.

But what about appearance? Appearance has to do with the body, just like happiness. Aren't they connected?

Appearance still refers to something outward. It's full label is, in fact, "Outward Appearance". Skin, hair, muscle, fat, these are surface level parts of the body. If we're talking about health, that's a different matter. Health refers to an inward experience in which you entire body is effected. It can therefore have an effect on systems responsible for releasing stress hormones. However, it's still possible to find peace in this situation through acceptance; it's still a choice.

I feel like spiritual books and some religious practices tell me it's wrong to want money and a nice house or car. But, I still want them and I don't think that's bad. I understand what you're saying. Still, I want to be happy and those things can help.

I don't think you're wrong, I think it's natural given the importance our society places on having "nice" things. Nice things are wonderful, it's the suffering we cause ourselves over attaining them that presents an issue. This conversation isn't about right or wrong, it's about feeling broken and what can bring you true happiness. If you feel broken because you don't drive a nice car, or because you're not like everyone else, then the happiness you seek is being thwarted by your point of view based on self-imposed comparisons. When we say, "I want money so I'll be happy," what we're really saying is, "I want to be happy and I think money will do that for me." If we can be open to the possibility of happiness being a state of mind and not a car in the driveway, then we can start to free ourselves from the chase; a chase that has made us unhappy while pursuing happiness.

3
TAKING THINGS PERSONALLY

I tend to take everything as a personal attack, even things that really have nothing to do with me. Someone can forget to call me and I'll think they may have done it on purpose. If someone goes around me in traffic or steals my parking space, it feels like they're trying to get the best of me. Things like that cause me a lot of suffering, how do I not take them so personally?

By just experiencing what is happening and trying not to label it as a personal attack.

But it feels personal, especially when someone is saying something directly to me.

That's understandable, especially when your beliefs about yourself are deeply embedded. "I'm strong" may be one you try to fortify. Thus, when anyone hints at the fact that you're weak, either through actions or words, you feel a need to defend yourself. It strikes a soft spot in you, raising an emotion, and you react to that emotion. The amazing part is, those soft spots are entirely self created. Therefore, the pain that you feel someone else is causing you, due to their actions or opinions, is really being caused by your own actions and opinions.

How so?

If you spend a lifetime convincing yourself that you're the best harmonica player in the world, and your entire identity and way of living comes from that stand point, you've just created an opportunity for others to challenge your opinion. That challenge, big or small, will make you defensive. After all, they're challenging your whole belief system. In your mind, the "fact" that you're the greatest harmonica player is not up for debate because it's an absolute truth, like the law of gravity or the sun being hot. Anyone expressing a different opinion is dead wrong. They have to be, it doesn't align with what you know to be true. If you try to present evidence of your truth or change their mind and they still don't believe you, it feels like they're personally attacking you. "They must be disagreeing with me on purpose because they don't like me or think I'm an idiot. Why else would they not agree with me, there's nothing wrong with me or what I'm saying? They're just being difficult. Either that or they're too stupid to understand that I'm the greatest harmonica player in the world. What's wrong with them? What a jerk." The story begins to weave itself very quickly about how you're right, they're wrong, and the world is against you. We can get so stuck on our opinions of how things should be, or of who we are, that we lose sight of the fact that they're only opinions we chose to invest energy into.

If they're just opinions, why do they cause pain? If they're not real, how do they cause a real emotion?

You've said it's real and so it becomes solid for as long as you believe it.

So, I'm not supposed to have an opinion about myself, or anything for that matter?

I didn't say that. You are entitled to believe what you'd like. Opinions make our experience of the world a more dynamic place. However, if you take a closer look at the things you take personally, the things that cause you suffering, you'll find that they're opinions you cling to wholeheartedly. If you choose to continue suffering, cling to the opinions as truths. If you choose to find a more peaceful way to interact with others, open to the idea that others are entitled to their opinions as well.

Even if those opinions say that my child is horrible or I'm incompetent?

Sure, why not? Perhaps from their view point you ARE incompetent or your child IS horrible. If you spend your time always defending your own opinions against everyone else's, you're going to find out very quickly that you have little time in the day for anything else. People's opinions are created from their own life experiences. If they had a father that drank and was abusive, they may look at someone's occasional beer as destructive and wrong. Thus, our past can create the lenses through which we view the world, lenses which are colored by opinions created by what we've experienced and how that affected us. When we see the world through these lenses we don't see reality, we only see our perception of it. If your sunglasses give the sun a bluish tint, does that really have anything to do with the sun? The more you can accept your opinions, and the opinions of others, as lenses instead of truth, the more easily you'll illuminate your own peace of mind, sun.

It's a shame we all fight over these petty things when it really seems to be a big miscommunication. I get so stuck in my views.

Well, that's where compassion comes in.

How so?

Being that we're all built to survive and thrive, the best way we can do that is through compassion and cooperation. If we all kill each other, how will we ever go on? History shows us that when we work together and show each other compassion, the human race - and the world for that matter - thrives. Thus, we're built to connect, cooperate, and help each other to some extent; that's our default. When someone is speaking to you in a hurtful way, they're not thinking of you, they're actually thinking of themselves. However, they're confused about what their hurtful comments are actually accomplishing. We know this to be true because if they understood what they were doing, they'd realize that talking to others in a hurtful way only perpetuates their own self-destructive anger and provokes an altercation, causing more of their own suffering. Why would they purposefully harm themselves when they're built to be compassionate?

Good question, I don't know.

Believe it or not, they ARE being compassionate. They're just going about it the wrong way. They're so wrapped up in their own pain that all they can think about is their desire to relieve it. A desire to relieve pain is an act of compassion. However, anything said or done out of this deep place of suffering is done illogically and selfishly. We're not bad people for doing this, we're just momentarily lost and scrambling to find a way out of the inner turmoil. An effective way to not take it personally is to see the experience for what it really is: A person in pain acting out. Let your compassion for someone in pain naturally arise. Let your compassion for feeling vulnerable after they've said something hurtful to you take care of your pain. Try to remember, you are not a concern of theirs, even though they're addressing you directly. Their only concern and focus at that point is themselves.

Seeing them with compassion when they're yelling in my face may be easier said than done.

It definitely is. I think it's perfectly natural to get defensive and want to strike back at some point. It's much easier to shut down or retaliate with anger because our feelings have been hurt. I think it helps to understand why we want to do that. At our core, we all want to connect with each other in some way. Those of us biologically capable of doing so seek this sense of belonging. When someone we had no ill intentions towards strikes out at us verbally, we momentarily feel sad. We may not have done anything to warrant that from them. Still, here they are saying things with the intention to cause us pain. This feeling of embarrassment for having allowed ourselves to be vulnerable, mixed with the feeling of betrayal and loss of belonging or connection, creates our sadness. It hurts. And, sometimes our first reaction when we're hurt is to shut down or retaliate with anger in order to stop any further pain from being inflicted upon us.

Why put ourselves in a position to feel that pain again? Why not just stay guarded?

I think that type of reasoning is behind the actions of some of the most closed down or cyclical people. "I'm just going to strike first or shut down completely, that way I can't be hurt like that again." That choice may not even be conscious at some point. It may be a subconscious habit learned after feeling pain over and over again. I believe some of the most closed down and aggressive people were at one time the most giving, caring, or compassionate ones. It's a shame they found themselves in a position of needing to shut down to survive. It separates them from experiencing the joy of connection. Vulnerability is necessary for a full human experience. That full experience also includes pain. Our fear of pain and a misunderstanding of the importance of vulnerability has created a society with a history of labeling it as "weakness".

So what do I do?

If you want to stop taking things personally, open up to the experience. Allow yourself the feel the pain and grow from it. Try to remember the pain is being exaggerated by your opinion that it was a personal attack; all you're feeling is the pain of being disconnected from someone. Try not to feed into the mind's tendency to create stories about the pain. Accept the discomfort with compassion by just experiencing it and not trying to chase it away or change it. Let it go through it's natural course and, in doing so, you'll be training yourself how to be more accepting and open. We believe that if we hunker down and put up walls around our hearts that we're protecting ourselves. But things that refuse to give an inch have a hard time surviving. We never see boxers standing in one place. The trees that don't bend with the wind break easily. The idea is to become open to change and emotions; to return to your awareness of what's happening, prior to thought and judgment. The more walls we put up, the easier it is for people to bang on them. The more walls we take down, the less places people have to bang on; you can't bang on space. The way we take the walls down is by experiencing the emotions without judgment and allowing them to train us to open up.

I don't say anything to the person that hurt me?

If you want to grow in a direction of openness from the experience, I think it can be healthy to express yourself. However, try do so from a place of understanding and honesty. It may be hard to admit to the other person that their actions caused you pain because this moves you into a place of vulnerability again. Taking that step can be greatly beneficial to you, but maybe you should only do so when you feel ready to handle whatever their response is. In the meantime, working on silently forgiving them can help you to move past it. Try to remember that they acted that way for a reason and that reason could very well be that at some point they were hurt too. This doesn't condone what they did. However, seeing it from another point of view can hopefully help you to move past feeling victimized and targeted. If we can start to look at people with compassion, focusing on the emotion behind their actions, then we can start to move away from the need to reference ourselves in the situation and thus the continual pain that causes. By understanding that our hurtful behaviors are driven by internal pain and our inability to skillfully cope with it, we can find greater peace within the things that we once took personally.

4
I'M NOT SPECIAL

Why don't I feel special? There's this underlying belief that I'm not good enough. Where did that come from?

Good question. It could have came from a number of places. But, you can be assured of one thing, it's a self-imposed belief; you weren't born with it.

What do you mean?

When you're born, you're free of beliefs about yourself. You're a squishy new body, some hair, and possess the awareness of things happening in and around you. Mix in some engrained directives in our spirit and genes and there you are. The rest gets programmed into our brain: Words, habits, beliefs. That's all a bunch of data we import.

I chose to believe I'm worthless?

We choose to keep believing it. Sometimes this choice is automatic. If we're already in the habit of living from the belief that we're worthless, then the choice to fulfill this belief through actions and words happens almost automatically and we just kind of run with it.

How does that work?

For example, let's take the thought about not being special. Let's say you just did something you're proud of. Then, you find yourself face to face with the reality that someone else did something similar and they're receiving praise for it. How do you typically feel in that situation?

I feel bad. I start questioning myself. Here I did something I was proud of and thought was pretty special. But then I see someone else did the same thing and maybe did it better. I feel like, no matter how hard I try, I'm never good enough and I have nothing that makes me special.

What do you do at that point?

I usually give up or lose any feeling of pride. I shut down.

Do you see how quickly it spiraled? You went from a moment of doubt to completely shutting down, thus strengthening your feeling of doubt and the belief that you aren't good enough. That all started with the flash of an emotion or thought. It was only a flash and you grabbed onto it, perpetuating it through continued actions and words representing self-doubt and worthlessness.

But that's how I feel. How do I deny how I feel?

That's how you THINK you feel, literally. All that happened was an emotion rose inside of you followed by a thought that aligned with the emotion. It would have passed, and you could have continued your day, had you not fed into it. Now, it's important to understand that your choice to feed into it happened so quickly that you didn't even realize you made a choice. It was more of a reflex due to training yourself over the years to respond in that way.

How do I choose to feel special then?

First, you have to acknowledge that your feelings of worthlessness are self-imposed. You won't be able to choose a new story, and effectively create a new habit, without first acknowledging that the old one is an illusion. If you continue to hold onto it as a core belief and absolute truth, you're going to have a very difficult time changing it. That's not to say it will completely disappear once you acknowledge it, but it loosens up your grip on it so you both can move on.

MY grip on it?

Of course. It's not gripping YOU. It's not sticking around because it wants to. It's sticking around because everything you do reinforces it. It's like the neighborhood cat. The more you feed him, the longer he sticks around waiting for food. As soon as you stop putting out kibble, he moves on. Acting worthless and repeating stories, mentally or to others, about how worthless you are is in effect feeding the belief and keeping it around. Stop putting out the kibble.

Ok, I agree that it's self-imposed. Now what?

Now you take a look at why you believe that. What is it about yourself that makes you think you're not special?

Because everyone else seems to be doing something important. A lot of people I know are successful or have a talent they excel at. They receive recognition for their accomplishments and skill sets. I don't have that anymore. I thought I did. But, there are so many people out there better or more talented than I am, I can't compete.

Who says you need to compete?

If I want to get ahead, I need to compete. If I want to be successful, I need to be better than the others.

It depends on your definition of success. If you've already established a belief that in order to be successful or special you need to be better than everyone else, then you've created your own cat and mouse game. You'll forever be chasing your idea of success because you'll always be thinking other people are better than you. In reality, you've concocted the whole thing! Nobody said you needed to be better than anyone else in order to be successful or happy, YOU created those rules. And, as if you didn't give yourself enough pressure, you decided that if you didn't meet these new self-imposed standards that you're worthless and could never meet them anyway. You literally believe that you're unable to live up to your own imaginary standards and punish yourself for it. You're losing a competition with yourself...because you said that you're too tough to compete with...now THAT's paradoxical.

And now I feel stupid.

I didn't mean to make you feel stupid, only to illuminate the reality of the scenario you find yourself in. It's difficult to find our way out of the maze, when we aren't even aware that we're inside of one to begin with. I only meant to show you the maze.

It's ok. I appreciate it.

What steps do you think you need to take now?

First, I need to stop creating such an impossible situation for myself. Then, I need to stop comparing myself to others.

There you go! Everyone is special because everyone is unique. Look no further than yourself to find an amazingly special, one-of-a-kind, human being. As far as talents, they're not meant to gain praise or status, they're meant as a means of connection and expression. Talents come in all shapes and sizes. Whatever you feel your talent is, continue to indulge in it. Is it not the act of expressing your talent that bring you happiness?

It is. I feel amazing when I lose myself in it. And, I feel horrible when I hope others will praise me for it but they don't.

Then why look any further for happiness or success than the act of losing yourself in it? Why continue to torture yourself?

I guess because I see other people making a living from their talent. I wish could do that as well. I tried, but couldn't do it.

Perhaps the talent you believe should earn you a living isn't the only talent you have. Perhaps you harbor another one that will earn you a living in the future. Or, perhaps you have yet to take the steps necessary to earn a living with your talent. Also, how do you define "making a living"? Would you be happy earning enough to survive without excess if you were able to do so using only your talent? Are you placing a time table on when you should be earning this living because you feel discomfort with your current situation? A time table that creates more unnecessary judgment against yourself and your life at this moment? In either case, success is defined by the individual. What definition of success can you adopt that ceases to cause you pain due to comparisons?

I could choose to believe that I'm successful because I found my talent and am able to express myself through it.

That is definitely a more peaceful definition. Financial success and success in life can be two very different things. There are many people who are financially successful but emotionally bankrupt. They're miserable; always chasing, always comparing, never happy. Then, there are people who earn a modest living and spend time doing what they love without the concern of financial success or approval of others. These people are emotionally successful, recouping their investment in themselves with tremendous returns. The question seems to be: Which person do you choose to become?

The second one.

Then cease the stories and live your truth. When you begin to compare or condemn yourself, stop. It's only you in there, why treat yourself so badly? Believe that you're special and choose your words and actions accordingly. It will take time, but slowly you can change your belief of worthlessness into a fortune of self-esteem and happiness.

"WHICH PERSON DO YOU CHOOSE TO BECOME?"

5
WORRY & FEAR

I'm tired of being paralyzed by my worry and fear.

Why does it paralyze you?

I get these thoughts that I can't do it or I will fail and the fear just rushes over me.

What do you mean by "*The fear just rushes over me*"?

I can feel it. I get scared. Or I feel sad.

What does that feel like?

What do you mean?

Well, when we feel cold we shiver. When we feel excited we can get little butterflies in our stomach and feel like we're full of energy. What does the fear or sadness feel like?

It's like a buzzing in my body. Or my thoughts can

become muddied or one tracked - repeating that I can't do it or that I'm scared.

Keep describing the sensations, please.

Sometimes my heart pounds or my breathing will get faster or heavy. I can feel this energy in me. It feels overwhelming at times. My stomach can get nauseas occasionally. Sweaty palms. At other times, the world can seem scary, like I just want to get out of there. Or I shut down and decide I don't want to do what I was trying to do because the thought of doing it makes me too afraid.

The thought of doing it or the thought of failing at doing it?

I suppose the thought of failing at it or something bad happening to me when I do it.

By "bad" do you mean anything other than what you want the result to be?

I suppose so.

And this energy in you - and it's various symptoms - you say it paralyzes you?

Yes.

Interesting.

Why is that interesting?

Because energy is typically thought of as movement or "umph". The fact that you use the term "energy" and say that it's paralyzing you seems to be contradictory.

But it does. I feel that stuff and then I don't want to keep going because it's making it worse.

Why do you think it's making it worse?

Because the more I do it the more I feel the energy in me. I don't like the way it feels.

Do you keep having thoughts that you're going to fail or something "bad" is going to happen the more you trying to accomplish this thing?

I'm not sure. I guess so, when I think back to different times it's happened.

Let me summarize, just to make sure I have all the information straight. There's this thing you want to do. For the sake of this conversation, let's say it's selling a creative project to the public. You are saying you want to do it, so that means you have an interest in really completing this task. Is that correct?

Yes.

And then you start to have thoughts that maybe it won't work or you're going to fail, is that correct?

Yes.

And then you start to feel this energy in your body that makes your heart beat or your skin sweat and generally you don't like this feeling. It scares you?

Yes. Sometimes that feeling will come up before I even think I'm gonna fail. Sometimes it comes up when I just think about doing something I want to do.

Okay. So, in both cases, this energy comes up in you and it seems to be linked to your conscious or subconscious fear of failing. Is that fair to say?

Yes.

And then, when you feel these sensations that you don't like, you shut down or stop what you're attempting to do in order to make those feelings go away. Is that also correct?

Yes. Especially if the more I try to accomplish my task the worse the sensations get. I'll just stop so I don't have to deal with it.

Okay. And lastly, do you believe these sensations or this energy of "fear" is directly linked to what you want to accomplish? In other words, do you think it's the thing you want to do that's causing you the fear?

I suppose so. Otherwise, why would the fear go away when I stop trying to do that particular thing?

That's exactly the question I hope to answer for you. First, let's get some perspective on what this energy we call "fear" really is. Energy is motion. That is why I find it interesting that you believe the energy you feel is paralyzing you. I can completely understand why it would feel like that. The energy can feel uncomfortable as it builds up. I believe it feels uncomfortable because the energy is intense and is looking for somewhere to go. Ultimately, the energy isn't paralyzing you, it's actually trying to get you to take action. The heart pounding, the heavy breathing, the sweating, these symptoms are similar to what we feel when we are working out or doing some sort of physical activity, are they not?

Yes, they are.

The difference is we aren't doing any sort of physical activity yet. But, our body is prepping us for it. It's getting us ready to move and do the things we need or want to do. It's revving up the engine.

But why is it doing that?

There's the million dollar question. It's doing it because it knows we need it. Remember the first question I asked when I was summarizing your statements?

You asked me if this all starts when there's

something I have an interest in doing.

Exactly. You have declared that you want to do something. Like most of us, it's probably something you truly want to accomplish, so much so that you can feel it in your heart and soul.

That's true. It's usually something I feel inspired to do.

So, you've set the stage. You've declared your goal.

Then why do I feel scared to do it?

Well, what you feel and what you think are two different things. What you feel is not fear, what you feel is energy. The thoughts you have are fearful. But that's doesn't mean the energy in you is one of fear.

So why does it happen when I start to worry then?

Because it's trying to give you the energy to push you through it. You've already decided what your heart wants to do. But, your mind and beliefs about your potential to do so are contradicting what your heart wants. So, your heart, body, soul, spirit kicks in to help you accomplish what you truly want to accomplish. It knows you've just put up a wall made of worry, doubt, disbelief, and fear. It knows that the wall can keep you from what you truly want to do so it revs you up. It rises to the occasion to stand by your side and it does this by giving you the energy you feel. That energy is yours to use as you wish. Just like a car engine revving up, the choice is yours to either put it in drive and crash through that wall or to put it in reverse and back away from it. Either way, that energy is waiting to be used.

If it wants me to crash through it, why does that feeling go away when I back away from it.

Because you've made another decision. You've decided that you don't want to do it right now. If you've decided you don't want to drive anymore, what's the point in revving the engine?

Ah. I see!

We get confused, believing that what we're feeling, the energy in us, is confirming our fearful thoughts. However, the energy is contesting the thought and actually giving us the power to push through it.

So, what do I do if I keep worrying while I'm trying to finish the task?

Keep using the energy to push through. Try to remember that what you're feeling is telling you that you can do it and giving you the strength to do so. To do this, focus on the energy instead of your thoughts. Thinking is an activity. You have to spend energy to partake in it, like moving your arm. Choose to not spend energy on thinking or perpetuating whatever fear based thoughts that may arise. Instead, refuse to make yourself suffer and choose to focus on the physical sensations of where you're at and what you're doing. If you find yourself sucked back into thinking, again, refuse to make yourself suffer and refocus. Ruminating is a habit, like biting your finger nails. Choose to not keep up the habit, it doesn't serve you well. Also, be kind to yourself. You care so much about what you're doing that you're concerned about doing it to the best of your ability and that's ok. It only becomes an issue when it stops you from doing what you truly want to do. We can't control every outcome. But, we can learn to control our response to it and enjoy the process of working towards a goal. That way, no matter what the end result is, we can look back at the good times we had and walk away feeling proud of even taking on the task.

Ok. So I use the energy to push though. What if the energy scares me?

Do you get scared when you feel excited?

No, I feel excited.

It's the same energy. The only difference is that we've labeled it as "scary" because we don't know why it's happening and that makes us feel uncomfortable. But, if we can look at it for what it really is - energy meant to help propel and guide us towards what we truly want - then the energy becomes a spark of inspiration and we can't wait to put our car in drive.

My Self

6
LONELINESS

I feel alone.

Why?

Because, the reality is, I'm the only one that wakes up as me in the morning and the only one who goes to bed as me at night. I'm the only one who experiences these difficult emotions inside of me. I was born alone. I die alone. And, look, I even talk to myself because it's just me.

I don't think you're right, but I can understand why you would feel like that.

Why don't you think I'm right?

For starters, it doesn't feel right. It feels painful to think that. It feels uncomfortable. It feels like a piece of clothing that just doesn't fit right. Do you feel good when you think that you're alone?

No.

That's because 1) You are making yourself feel disconnected and we are built to be connected beings, and 2) That thought doesn't align with what's really in your spirit. The bad feeling isn't confirming your thought, it's contesting it.

I never thought of it that way.

Let's look at the reasons you feel alone. You're not the only one that wakes up. Billions of people wake up. Animals wake up. At any given moment, you're probably waking up at the exact same time thousands of other people are.

But, they don't wake up as me.

You want a thousand "you's"?

No.

Then, why would you be upset that you're the only one waking up as you?

I just mean that I go through life as me and I do it alone. I see the world through my eyes, nobody else sees it with my eyes. I feel these fears and think these thoughts in my head, no one else is thinking them or experiencing them. That's what I mean by alone. It's just me and I don't like it. It's lonely.

First, seeing through a pair of eyes is not an experience unique to you. Billions of people have the exact same experience. Feelings of fear or strong emotions aren't unique to you either. Billions of people feel those exact same emotions. And, they may think it's unique to them too, especially when what they're feeling at the moment is painful. But, at any given time, there are at least a thousand people in the world feeling the exact same emotion that you are because emotions are universal. Fear or sadness are not solely YOUR fear or sadness, they're the same emotions that your neighbor or a factory worker in another country is capable of feeling. Therefore, you're sharing your emotional experience with people all across this beautiful earth. The act of thinking is also universal. So, you can bet that billions of people are sharing your experience of thinking at any given moment. You may feel alone, but you're very much connected to everyone by these experiences that make us human. You weren't born alone, your mother was right there with you. You don't die alone because thousands of people are experiencing the same transition at the same time that you are. Thinking that you're alone creates a feeling of discomfort because it's a belief that is very much the opposite of what you intuitively know. Even as you walk in the desert, the desert is walking with you. The sand is holding you up. The sun is giving you Vitamin D. You're inhaling oxygen created by a plant in some other part of the world and exhaling carbon dioxide that will feed a different one. They're with you as well. When you wake up, your heart is with you. In fact, while you were sound asleep, your heart, lungs, and Central Nervous System, guided by an unknown amazing intelligence, stayed awake watching over you; taking care of you so that you could wake up in the morning. While the drool slowly soaked into your pillow, your immune system worked diligently to bring your body back into balance. They're with you at all times, taking care of you like the a gentle compassionate parent. You are never alone. And, if it's connection with others you seek, you only need to make the effort because at any given time there are people feeling alone, hoping someone would connect with them. Lastly, as far as talking to yourself goes, it's a miracle of life. It's the hallmark of self-awareness. Your ability to talk to yourself gives you the chance to experience yourself, to get to know yourself, to offer support to yourself in hard times, to create, to explore, to connect. You have the potential to be your own best friend and greatest supporter as you cheer yourself on through challenges and console yourself during hard times. Those that take the time to talk to themselves are building a vital relationship that can help them to flourish and feel fulfilled. It's true, if you don't share your thoughts with others they may never know the exact content, or get a chance to relate to them, because your thoughts are occurring in your mind. But, since you're aware of them, you can address them. You can expand on or dismiss them. You are never alone because you have yourself and that's an amazing gift! Give me one example of a time that you're not connected to something or someone else by experience.

I can't think of one when you put it that way.

I'm not putting it any way, I'm simply stating how it is without the imposed storyline of being alone. It's understandable to feel alone sometimes, especially when circumstances are very challenging and you want nothing more than for someone to be with you as you go through them. Heck, sometimes we wish others could go through them for us. But, the reality is that people ARE going through them with us and people HAVE gone through them before us. A good number of those people have shared their experiences, hoping to save us from the pain, or at least to let us know that we're not alone in our struggles. You are not alone, no matter how much it may feel like it. At the very least, you have yourself and you always have your best intentions in mind, even if you express it in a unhelpful way.

So what do I do now?

Connect. Look at the world around you and within you, thinking of the many wonderful ways that you're connected to it. Think of the ways it supports you and how you're very much in a relationship with everything and everyone around you. Even if they don't know it or acknowledge it, these people you call "strangers" are your extended family; you all count on each other in some way, shape, or form. Start embracing that. Find the magic in that. And, when you're feeling alone, remind yourself that there are people all across the world feeling the exact same way at the exact same time that you are. It's the amazing gift of experience that connects you. Embrace the connections, embrace yourself, and be grateful you have the opportunity to do so.

"YOU ARE NOT ALONE, NO MATTER HOW MUCH IT MAY FEEL LIKE IT."

7
SUFFERING

There's so much suffering in myself and around the world. Why do we suffer?

Are you talking about emotional suffering?

Yes.

Denial of reality.

How do we deny reality?

By creating stories about it that are trying to avoid it or cling to it.

Can you give me some examples?

If someone breaks up with you, you may create a story that says, "I'm no good. They broke up with me because I'm worthless." Or, you may try to deny that they broke up with you, avoiding the pain of it by getting drunk or dating other people quickly in order to forget about your ex. Lastly, you may cling onto someone who is trying to take a different direction in their life. You may call them constantly, begging for them to come back even though it's clearly evident your relationship was toxic. You may find yourself depressed or irate as you cling to memories of happier times and can't accept that those times are gone. You may even offer to change fundamental things about your life, such as your hobbies or friends, just to make them happy so you can hang onto the relationship. That is all a denial of reality. And, that all creates suffering.

Why do we do that?

Fear of change or the unknown. We become comfortable in knowing that everything has its place. When the order of things is challenged, we tend to view it as a sign that something is wrong. We work so hard to keep everything under control that the slightest situation that arises outside of our control creates worry and fear. Suffering is caused by the denial of reality, which is to say the denial of the fact that everything is always changing. We grow to love the predictable so much that even when our comfort zone is causing us pain, we still prefer it to the unknown.

Everything is always changing?

Is it not?

But, don't we have the ability to control some things and keep them the same?

Only one, your choice of action or reaction to that which is always changing. All else is a story you have told yourself about how you think reality should be. Suffering is created by the mind in an attempt to avoid suffering. It's yet another thing that is paradoxical.

I suffer because I don't want to suffer?

You suffer because you don't know the difference sometimes. The mind attempts to interpret an experience by connecting dots of information stored in its memory. These dots, which can be random and vaguely connected to what you're experiencing, flash in your mind as images or words. You then take these dots and weave stories about your experience. For example, if you're experiencing slight discomfort in your chest and two months ago you read an article about somebody having a heart attack, that story, or dot, may flash in your mind. If you have a tendency to automatically cling to these dots, you may create a story about the discomfort actually being a sign of cardiac arrest and send yourself into a panic. However, five minutes later, you burp and feel fine. Depending on your deep-seeded beliefs, and the information you've taken in over the years, these stories could very much be about how you need to get a grip on your circumstances in order to be safe; "I need more money", "I need to look better", "I don't feel right, I need to fix that." Too often, we get wrapped up in these stories, mistaking them as truth, especially if they frighten us. We start believing that we really DO need more money or that something really IS wrong with us, so we scramble in order to address whatever the story says we need to fix. All of this is an attempt to avoid the suffering that the stories say we'll face if these issues aren't resolved. However, the scrambling itself causes us great anxiety and suffering. The chase of trying to fix everything is exhausting and futile because the things we need to resolve are imaginary to begin with; they're only stories we created out of random dots. We're chasing ghosts! In essence, we create suffering in an attempt to avoid suffering, suffering that only existed because we said it did.

But aren't there times when we DO need more money or need to fix ourselves?

Sure. And when that reality is accepted then it doesn't create suffering, it creates forward momentum. There are many examples of people working difficult jobs for long hours who do what is necessary and feel accomplished for doing so. They don't create stories that fight with reality. Thus, they feel a sense of ease about it, even gratitude for the opportunity to be alive rather than cursing life for their circumstances. It's only when you perpetuate unhelpful storylines about your reality, and then ruminate over them, that you suffer.

Wow. Why do we torture ourselves like that?

Again, because you don't know that you're doing it. You don't know that you've created this scenario, you only know that something's telling you to scramble and fix your life. You get glimpses of the truth when you say things like, "Why do I care so much?", or "Why am I acting like this?" Part of you knows the scramble is causing you pain, but you still haven't had a chance to fully realize what's happening. It isn't until you reach a point where scrambling to control everything creates so much suffering that you decide enough is enough. Only then do you begin to challenge your need for control and accept reality for what it is. That's when an energy rises in you and much is accomplished. You begin working with circumstances that arise as opposed to complaining about them. Have you ever had a time when you dropped the storylines and solely focused on getting something done?

Yes, when I was putting together a charity event.

What was the result?

It got done.

And how did you feel?

Great. Powerful.

Was there any suffering?

No. I only felt energized to finish what I set out to do. I was focused on getting it done.

It's amazing what the absence of our stories can do for our well being and productivity.

Is there a deeper purpose for suffering? It seems useless.

It depends on how you look at it. As human beings, we need the contrast to fully know and enjoy our experience. We also need it to survive and thrive. Suffering serves as a catalyst. Some people need only hints of suffering to move in a more joyful direction. Others need greater degrees of suffering before they make a change. Suffering serves to push us in the direction of expanded experience and deeper connection, both to ourselves and those around us. Without it, compassion couldn't arise. When someone is crying, others feel compelled to console them. That suffering opened the door for connection, which is need if we're to survive and thrive as a species. If we felt emotionally flat or content all the time, with neither suffering nor compassion, what would drive us to connect with each other? We'd be sitting on the grass by ourselves, without the need for interaction with others, staring at the sky. How could we possibly continue as a species that way and fulfill our purpose in nature or the Universe?

What IS our purpose?

That's a great question for another time. For now, do you have a better understand suffering?

I believe so. It help us connect with each other.

Exactly. It's not a punishment, it's a necessary

component that helps drive life. However, the choice is yours in regards to how much suffering you want to experience. When it arises, see if you can notice the compassion that arises with it. You may find it in the form of trying to ease your suffering. You may see it in children when they offer their toy to a friend who is crying. Seek to observe the beautiful energy that arises out of suffering and not only will it take on a new meaning for you, it'll help to open your heart as well, making life a much more enjoyable experience regardless of the circumstances.

> "IT'S ONLY WHEN YOU PERPETUATE UNHELPFUL STORYLINES ABOUT YOUR REALITY, AND THEN RUMINATE OVER THEM, THAT YOU SUFFER."

8
TRUSTING MY SELF

I don't trust myself.

What do you mean?

I don't trust my mind, my body, myself to be ok.

Why?

Because at some point I felt like my mind was torturing me. My body too.

How so?

I developed really bad anxiety and my body got weak. I couldn't eat and had no strength. It happened out of nowhere. I was fine, living my life, and chasing my dream and all of the sudden I began having panic attacks. My heart started skipping beats throughout the day. I'd have chest pains. Then, I couldn't eat. I lost nearly 30 pounds in a little over a month. I'd wake up and the first thing I'd feel was a wave of panic. My mind was always thinking worrisome thoughts. I began to fear for my health and my life. I was being tortured.

Do you still feel that way?

I guess a part of me is still always expecting something to happen, either my mind to get anxious or my body to give out. Everything will be perfectly fine and the fact that it's fine makes me start to wonder if my mind or body are gonna do something to make it not fine. It seems like I'm always on high alert. I just want to trust myself again. How do I do that?

By choosing to.

Is that it?

That's where it starts. Even though it was a decision that happened quickly, you chose to not trust your mind or body. Part of you, the true you, observed that something inside of you was drastically different. Understandably, you assumed these new painful experiences meant that you were "in trouble", thus choosing to not trust your mind or body; the source of your pain. Over time, you've reinforced this choice by always keeping an eye on them and waiting for the worst to happen. We condition ourselves to expect the worst so we feel better prepared for it. That preparation gives us a false sense of security. In reality, the expectation is what actually causes the distress to occur.

So what do I do?

Choose to trust that your mind and body are not attacking you. Choose to believe that these things happened as a result of circumstances coming together that caused your mind and body to respond in that way. And, that when these circumstances change so does the response. It's the basic law of cause and effect, it wasn't punishment. It wasn't because you were in "trouble". It was simply what occurred as a result of what happened prior to it. If you accidentally let go of a balloon and it floats up and away from you, was that punishment? No. It was simply the result of accidentally letting go. Does that makes sense?

Yes.

As we talked about before, your mind is constantly seeking safety by connecting random dots and bits of information stored in your brain. This can result in worrisome thoughts. These worrisome thoughts do not even need to be accurate, they're just a product of imagination and information gathered over the years. Your body responds to these thoughts according to what type of energy you give them. Your body creating a lack of appetite, and thus losing weight, was a result of its heightened state of stress; the hormones and physiological changes that come along with it. It wasn't punishment or a purposeful torment. However, isn't it interesting that you recognized there was a "you" being "tortured"?

What do you mean?

We can address that another time. But, it's important and rather insightful. However, I will say that the because "you" felt tortured, you then chose to rally up another part of you that stood on guard at all times to keep "you" safe. That sounds terribly exhausting.

It is. I feel mentally exhausted from always having to check in on myself and wonder about my state of mind or body.

That's interesting too. Why do you think that you "Always have to check in with yourself"?

Because if I don't...actually...I don't know. I guess it makes me feel safe because if I keep an eye on it then I can do something about it if I need to.

What do you think you can do about it?

Well, at this point I work on trying not to get sucked into it.

"It" being the anxiety, worry, or discomfort in your body that you mentioned earlier?

Yeah. Now, I try to just let it be. I try to recognize that it's just passing through as I focus back on my breath like I learned when studying mindfulness.

So, the times that you feel panic or worry, you try to just let it go. But, the times that you don't feel worried, you worry about being worried so you're ready to just let it go?

...I suppose so.

When everything's alright, you expect it to not be alright so you can make it alright again, which you then make not alright by expecting it to not be alright. When can anything ever be alright like that?

I never thought of it like that.

That DOES sound exhausting. That seems to be the equivalent of always rallying up the troops only to tell them there's no fight, that you just wanted to make sure they're ready. So, they go back to their bunkers. And, as soon as the area is clear and calm, you rally the troops again. Don't you see, you have to actually choose to put effort into rallying the troops. Otherwise, it's naturally calm. You're not creating a safer environment, you're creating one filled with tension and choosing to expend energy to do so.

But if I don't, and my mind and body go into those panicky reactions again, I'll be caught off guard and caught up in it like I was before.

You're already caught up in it. The fact that you're always on guard means you're caught up in it. If you're always guarding against it, you haven't let it go. Isn't that true?

I suppose so.

Think of all the times you were cautious about what you were feeling, where you were going, or what was happening. All that caution, all that guarding, and you STILL had no freedom or peace. You still were caught in the storm of panic, fear, and worry. I'd say always being on guard didn't serve you well.

At least I knew it was coming.

How do you know that you weren't actually calling it to you by waiting so intently for it to happen?

Are you saying I caused this?

On some level, you may have prolonged it for much longer than needed. Really, it's not a matter of not trusting yourself. You can very much trust your mind and body to react in the way you expect it to.

If I didn't expect it, it wouldn't happen, but because I expect it to happen then it does?

Things may still happen because of outside situations you interact with. But, expecting yourself to go into panic or distress during those situations already tells your body and mind how you want to react to it. The power is in your hands to act or react the way you want to. You don't trust your body and mind but they're not your enemy and they're certainly not plotting against you. They're simply doing what they need to do and what you've trained them to do. You've trained your dog to roll over for food, and then began to distrust him for rolling over. How much more must your body and mind do to gain your trust? If you don't want your dog to roll over, stop telling him to and teach him a new trick.

Interesting.

Very.

I'd like to trust myself again. I feel like it's torn me apart not to.

Of course you do, there's a division within yourself. There's you, the side on guard, and there's your mind and body, the perceived tormentors. You're walking around scared of yourself. When can you ever rest?

I get some relaxation when I'm making or listening to music, writing, watching a movie, things like that; when I'm doing things I'm interested in.

That's interesting too.

What is?

That your problems and nervousness about yourself seem to magically go away when you're doing something else.

Why is that interesting?

If your fear were something solid, unmoving, and real, don't you think it would always be there regardless of what you're doing? Isn't it strange that it just disappears when you don't focus on it and reappears when you do?

I've never considered it gone.

Of course not, you're always looking for it.

What I mean is that I always assumed it was still there. I just wasn't focusing on it so I didn't notice it, like a person standing next to me. I can ignore the person, it doesn't mean they're gone.

This is true. But, a person is not an emotion or a thought. For the sake of this conversation, a person is solid. A thought or emotion rises and falls. Emotions shift into different forms, such as anger or joy, and a thought disappears as quickly as it comes. Each word vanishes into space as its being "said" in your mind. These things rely on your focus for their continued existence after they've run their initial course. And, the fact that they disappear when you don't pay attention to them proves that. Tell me, have you ever lifted weights?

Yes.

Bench press?

Yes.

Ever lower the bar to your chest and then try to push it up but it was too heavy so you only end up grunting and shaking, bearing the weight but unable to move it?

That's happened a couple of times. Luckily there was a spotter.

If you ignored the weight, started singing a song in your head, or watching the TV in the gym, do you think the weight would disappear?

Of course not.

Exactly. It's not going to disappear just because you read a book. But, somehow, the fear and worry does. There must be a difference between the two examples. What do you think it is?

The weight doesn't need my attention to continue existing, the fear does.

Exactly. It's somehow being created by focusing on it, even if it's indirectly. If I say, "I'm afraid," and "I don't want to be afraid," am I not still mentioning the word "afraid" and therefore focusing on it? Consequently, it's dispersed by your LACK of focus. Build trust in your body and mind again by ceasing to create excessive worry that wasn't there initially, allowing it to react in non-fearful ways.

How do you cease from creating excessive worry?

By letting go of the worry because it's not helpful or logical?

Exactly. And how do you do that?

By focusing on something else?

Yes! You can even focus on the sensations of the emotion itself, just drop the storylines about them. And, if there are no emotions, then focus on what you're doing. When you start to worry, go back to what your senses are feeling and drop the storylines again. You're retraining your mind to relax whenever something that initially made you worry arises. You can do this because you are not your thoughts, you are not even the sensations. That stuff is just passing through, so let it. Do that and you'll see that you're not broken and there's nothing to distrust. You're a beautiful process of flowing energy and part of a system with a body and mind that are ever changing and evolving, that allows you to experience your existence. They're your friends, collaborating with you and helping you discover and engage in this amazing world. Be grateful for their friendship.

That sounds wonderful, I will do my best. I have one question though: What did you mean when you said that I'm not my thoughts or sensations?

That's a great question, and we'll get to that soon.

9
LETTING GO
(CONTROL)

I'm scared of letting go.

What do you mean?

I'm scared to let things be as they are. Some things don't feel so great or seem like they're going to lead to a lot of heartache and pain if I let them run their course.

Some things don't feel great and some things may lead to heartache. Why would you want to hold on to them any longer than you have to?

It's not that I want to hold on to them, I want to stop them from happening or from losing control of keeping things together. I'm scared of what will happen if I do.

This seems to be a running theme in your questions.

Is it?

Isn't it?

The need for control?

Absolutely. You seem to have this strange idea that you can control everything that is happening inside and outside of you.

I can control some of it.

Can you? Can you really control it or is that something you've convinced yourself of and that's why you keep trying to do so?

I'd have to think about it.

Thinking about it may lead you to the same answer, since it's what created the answer in the first place. Perhaps you should trying "feeling" about it instead.

What do you mean?

Thinking tends to create more stories, even if they're stories about how your previous stories aren't correct. Observing and feeling the situation deals with things as they are, without any distortion. Feel your way through it.

How do I do that?

First, you have to decide that you want to let go. I think you've already made that decision, otherwise, we wouldn't be having this conversation. Some part of you knows that trying to control everything is only making you suffer.

How do you know that?

You're telling me that you're scared of letting go which infers that you want to. You wouldn't want to unless you thought it offered some benefit. So, to reap the benefit we have to determine what is causing your fear of letting go. In this case, the fear is created by the stories we tell ourselves about needing to stay in control, nothing more. Therefore, because you want the freedom of letting go, these stories that are convincing you to do otherwise are keeping you from that freedom and actually making you suffer, are they not?

I suppose they are.

So decide to let them go. They served a purpose at one time, but that time is over. When you start thinking of a reason to not let go, mentally label it as "thinking" and go back to feeling what's going on inside and around your body; come to your senses. This disregards the story and connects you directly and openly with what's happening. This sounds familiar, doesn't it?

It does. You've mentioned something like this during other conversations.

For good reason. Experience is your purpose. When you try to avoid experiencing the moment, you end up fighting yourself.

So, after I say, "Thinking," and go back to feeling what's happening, what do I do?

You roll with the experience.

How so?

By continuing to feel.

That sounds like I'm just gonna be a bottle in the ocean getting tossed and toppled by life.

I can see why you'd say that, but it's not quite the same thing.

How's it different?

You're not a bottle.

Very funny.

You're not. A bottle will toss and topple with the waves, content with the ride and where it ends up. A bottle can just be a bottle. It doesn't try to be a ship navigating the seas or a shark searching for food. You, however, keep trying to control the ocean. For some reason, you're under impression that being a bottle isn't good enough and that the ocean has no idea what it's doing. Yet, it sustained life without your help for billions of years and will continue to do so after you're gone. No, you are not a bottle.

I'm just supposed to sit back and let life toss me around without any say so about it?

Do you think you've had any say so up until now?

Some, yeah.

Really? Then how come, despite all of your efforts to control everything, you still end up here, scared, being tossed around?

...(silence)

You see, you've only created the illusion of complete control. It takes nothing more than an honest look at your life to see that the only control you ever had was the way you chose to react to a situation. Life happens, that's just the way it is. Your heart beats and stops on its own. Your brain releases chemicals when it needs to. And, the job you wanted so badly gets handed to the person you feel didn't deserve it no matter how much you kick and scream about it. The ONLY control you have is the choice you make regarding the way you handle life unfolding before you. Sure, you can choose to go workout or drink water instead of coffee tomorrow morning. But, you still can't control if the machine at the gym is out of order when you get there or if the water filter breaks as you fill up your glass. Letting go of your need for control isn't stepping into the unknown, it's stepping into the reality of life from the illusion of how you thought life worked.

That makes me feel so helpless.

How so?

It makes me feel like I HAVE to go with the flow and so I may end up doing things I don't agree with.

Give me an example, please.

Okay, let's say I have been working so hard at getting my business up and running. I truly believe in my product and I have a great marketing plan. It's something I'm really passionate about. What if I hit obstacles that seem to keep me from being able to sell my product, like stores not initially being receptive or running out of marketing funds? Am I supposed to throw my hands up and say, "Oh well, I should just go with the flow and quit because life is making it hard to sell my product"?

What would you typically do in that scenario?

I'd fight. I'd say, "It's go time!" and work harder. If the stores aren't buying it, I'd knock louder until they paid attention. If the funds aren't there, I'd work longer hours in order to afford the marketing. I wouldn't stop, I wouldn't take "no" for an answer. I don't care how much time and effort or lack of sleep it took, I'd get it done.

Do you think that would work?

I think it would work better than sitting back and waiting for life to give me the answers. Sitting on my couch isn't going to get anything done.

This is true. But, you're assuming that life wasn't already trying to give you the answers and direction you needed.

By making the stores not buy it and emptying my bank account?

And here in lies the problem with thinking that you can control everything that happens and that when things don't go your way they must be working against you. If you have something in your heart that you feel inexplicably excited about pursuing, then pursue it. That's life giving you a clue. Do you think YOU put that excitement in your body and mind? If you honestly look back at that initial spark of interest, didn't it just kind of come to you without you doing anything? Most people call it the "light bulb moment".

It did seem to kind of pop up. It was like an energy in me saying, "This is great, you should do it!"

So here you are, pursuing your dream and life gets in the way by making the store not buy your product. You decide you're going to fight with reality and force them to buy it. How much stress and heartache does that cause you? What happens if they still don't buy it?

It would be stressful, but at least I tried.

Sure, you tried. You can try to boil water with your heat vision too. It may not work, but at least you tried.

What do you mean?

If you're staring at the pot, really trying to get that water to boil using only your superpowers and it doesn't work, what are you going to do?

First, I'm going to laugh at myself. Then, I'm going to turn on the stove.

Why?

Because I'm not Superman.

Why else?

Because it wasn't working and I'd like to boil my noodles now.

It wasn't working. You didn't sit there and argue with the water or condemn yourself because you lacked the proper heat vision abilities to make it boil. Life let you know that your way wasn't going to work so you tried another way. You let go of trying to control the situation, and of any fixed ideas about how it should be, and you rolled with the waves. And, what do you know, the water still got boiled.

LETTING GO

So you're saying I shouldn't fight the stores?

I'm saying that having a plan and relentlessly carrying through with it despite what life is trying to tell you can be stressful and unproductive. I'm also saying that when life doesn't go the way you want it to, it doesn't mean that you still can't get what you want. You may have to be open to another way or a different version of your initial goal. We get so convinced that we're right, we refuse to consider other options; options that can still get the job done while causing us less stress in the meantime. You get stuck on your idea of what should be and when it doesn't coincide with your vision of everything in a safe and orderly fashion you fight it due to fear; specifically fear of the unknown. But your attempts to keep yourself safe aren't working, they're backfiring. Look at how stressed you are. Stop staring at the water, let go and turn on the stove.

What's the point in fighting the tides.

Exactly. Life flows through you, the same life powering your muscles or breathing your lungs. You're a vessel, like a water hose. The hose makes no effort to change or deny the water coming through it, it's content to be the vessel that helps life flow. Sure, sometimes conditions may twist the hose into knots and stop the stream. But, doesn't it get cracked and frayed when it's twisted? Life is always flowing through you. Let it flow and enjoy.

But I'm not a hose, I'm a human.

A hose with muscles and the ability to make choices. Unlike the hose, you tie yourself in knots. But, the water's still there ready to flow.

How do I untie myself and let it flow?

Pay attention to where you're resisting life. Pay attention to the tides and where they're leading you. Be open to the idea that maybe they're taking you somewhere better than you planned for. Fighting reality is a waste of energy because it's going to keep being reality anyway. Choose to drop the stories and go back to feeling your way through it. If it feels right to knock on the door of those stores one more time, do it. If it feels wrong, but your mind is telling you that you should, don't. Open up and look at the other options until one feels right. Aren't you tried of fighting? Aren't you tried of suffering from trying to control everything? Aren't you tired of doing that to yourself?

I am.

Then, stop. Stop torturing yourself. Let go. You're here anyway. Life is happening anyway. The best use of your energy is to find peace within life, not in spite of it. And, that all starts by letting go of trying to control it.

Thank you.

I AM

10
WHO AM I?
(MY TRUE SELF)

Who am I, really? You mentioned I'm not my thoughts or sensations. So, who am I?

"Who" is a funny term. Perhaps a better question is, "What are you?"

Ok, what am I?

Consciousness.

I've heard that term but don't fully understand what it means.

How have you heard it?

When someone is knocked out we say they're unconscious and when they wake up we say they're conscious. People also use it when they say someone is conscious, or aware, of something.

It can be roughly the same interpretation used to understand consciousness. Consciousness includes awareness. If someone is knocked out, they're not aware of what's going on, supposedly. When they wake up, they're thought of as being aware again.

Exactly.

Consciousness is partially awareness. It also consists of the power of intention and is driven by factors that help it to know its existence. You are consciousness, or awareness, which is constructed out of energy.

I'm awareness?

Very much so.

But I'm also human too, right?

Of course. You're consciousness in the form of a human.

Can you explain that, what exactly do you mean by awareness?

Let's start by asking some basic yes or no questions. These will help strip down the things we often come to believe are "us" and reveal your true self. Are you ready?

Yes.

If I took away your name, would you still be you?

I suppose so.

If I took away your job or status in society, would you still be aware that you're you?

Aware that I'm me?

Yes, if I took away your job and status would you still be able to know that you exist in this world? Would you be aware of that?

Yes.

What if you lost a limb? Perhaps all of them? Would you still be you?

I wouldn't feel like me, I'd feel different.

That's because you associate yourself entirely with your body. However, your body is something you coexist with. Think about it, imagine yourself without limbs. Would you still be you?

I guess I would be. A different version of me.

Would you still be aware that you're you?

Yes.

What if I took away your vision? Would you still be aware that you're you?

Yes.

Hearing?

It would be awfully quiet in here, but I suppose so. There are times when I've had my eyes closed and ear plugs in because I wanted silence so I could rest. I was still "there", whatever "there" is.

You were still aware.

Yes.

How about if I took away your ability to speak?

When I meditate, I'm silent. And, I'm very much aware of myself.

So then the question becomes: If you are still aware of yourself, of your presence, when we take away these things, including your senses, what are you?

I'm the one that's aware of my presence.

Exactly.

But don't I need my senses?

Have you ever heard of a sensory deprivation tank?

Yes. That's where people get in this cocoon looking tub and they can't feel anything.

Right. Not only can they not feel their body, they can't see or hear anything either. And yet, the person is still aware of their presence. But what are they aware of?

Themselves?

Since there are no senses to reference, people report their mind creating images or sounds for a short while. Then, after 15 - 30 minutes or so, the mind becomes silent as well. What they are left with is their true selves, their presence, awareness, consciousness.

But how do I know I'm "me" if I'm just this awareness?

"Me" is a term we use to refer to everything we experience as our mind and body. When you say, "I'm hungry," you're referring to your awareness of your body being hungry and the sensations that causes. Take away your body, such as in a sensory deprivation tank, and what do you have left to call "me"?

Nothing, I suppose. I'd just be there, aware.

Exactly. You're not aware of "you", you're aware of everything you refer to as "you" - mind and body. You are just awareness, consciousness, experience. Isn't it interesting that babies don't need to refer to themselves as "I", or using any language at all, in order to experience the world?

What do you mean?

Well, a baby comes out of the womb taking in all of this input from the world. You can see their inquisitiveness when they look at things. There are no labels or stories created about anything yet, there's only experience. It's pure. They don't know what an "I" is and yet they can experience the world and the sensations they feel. It seems that referencing ourselves is not necessary for experience. Animals aren't generally known to reference themselves, yet they're able to function and enjoy life. It seems they're simply aware of what's happening and respond to it accordingly. What's happening is just happening and that's the end of it. Awareness, then, is the baseline for our existence and what we truly are. The rest stems from this awareness.

Interesting.

To further illustrate this point, there is a famous neuroanatomist that suffered a stroke and wrote a book about her experience. The stroke temporarily took away her language center, which is also responsible for the reference of "I". She described her experience as euphoric and was unable to tell where she ended and the world around her began. She was purely aware of her presence and that everything was a part of her as she was a part of it. Her reference of self, and thus the view point of being separate from everything, disappeared and her true self emerged: consciousness. Without reference to self, you are just experience. You experience this and then move on to the next experience of that. Isn't it interesting that, just like babies and animals, she was still able to experience the world with euphoria when any reference to "I" disappeared? And yet those of us constantly referencing "I" seem to have the most suffering.

It is.

What does that confirm?

That we are not the "I" we call ourselves. We don't need the "I". The "I" holds us back.

It can hold you back, but it doesn't have to. You see, without the "I", or any experience for that matter, you couldn't experience yourself.

How so?

If all that you are is presence, or awareness, what would there be to experience?

I don't understand.

Take space, for example. Space is infinite, is it not?

It is.

Let's say there were no planets, only space. How could it know it's space if all there is is space? There's no reference point. It's awareness, but has no idea what it is or what it's capable of. It's saying,

"I'm here, but I have no idea what 'I' or 'here' is." It only knows it's presence, like a person in a sensory deprivation tank. If the person never left the tank, what could they ever experience besides their presence? It needs something else that it can reference against itself in order to know what it is. It needs something different in order to know the difference. When walls are built in a house, the walls give space a reference. Space can then say, "That's different, it's not me. I stop when I hit those things (walls). I must be everything in between these walls."

I think I understand. It's still slightly confusing.

Let's see if we can find a better example. Think of a kid that feels like an outcast at school. This kid can sense that she doesn't fit in with the popular crowd. Those kids dress different and they have different interests. She always wears black and they always wear pastels. They love football and parties and she loves video games and reading. How can she tell the difference between herself and the other kids?

Because they're different than she is.

Exactly. Let's say all of the kids started dressing in black clothes, playing video games, and reading. Would the kid know the difference between herself and the others?

No.

Why?

Because it's all the same now.

So how could she know her individuality and enjoy that experience if everything's the same?

She couldn't.

Do you understand now?

I do. Everything that is not us allows us to know ourselves.

Exactly. And since you are truly awareness, or consciousness, everything you experience, including the "I", allows you to know that you are the awareness experiencing it. You instinctively know the difference. That why we say things like, "I don't feel like myself today," or "My mind keeps racing." You reference everything as something you're observing or aware of. How could you only be the mind, or thoughts, if you're observing it? How could you be the sensation of not feeling like yourself if you're observing the sensation? When you're observing the television, are you the TV? You must, then, be the observer or the awareness experiencing it.

I am going to have to sit with that for a while. I have never thought about myself in that way before. I mean, you're right. It makes sense. It's just a drastically different way of thinking about myself.

For many reasons, it's a necessary way at this point in our evolution as beings. As we talked about at another time, so much suffering is caused because we tend to think that we ARE these emotions or thoughts. We identify completely with them and thus we operate from their standpoint. But, they are not meant for that. They're meant to be experiences and nothing more. They serve their purpose and move on. Thinking is just the brain connecting dots, replaying information, helping imagine new scenarios based on old ones, and trying to make sense out of your experiences. The body's emotions are just energy flowing and reacting to other energies. You are the one aware of it all. Again, that's why you can reference it and say, "I feel so angry." If you were solely the anger, how would you know the difference? Think of the kid dressed in black.

I wouldn't. I wouldn't be able to tell the difference between the anger and what I could be or was previously.

Exactly. There would be no reference point. Now, do you remember that I also said you have the power of intent? That consciousness is awareness AND intention?

Yes.

This is where your power of intention comes in. It gives you the freedom of choice. You get to chose where to focus your energy and expression. And the reason you get to use your power of intention is because you have things to reference. If anger didn't arise you couldn't have an intention to be peaceful. So, the experiences you have give rise to your power of intention, they fuel it. If you're sitting on the couch and a TV commercial comes on that you don't like, are you aware of it?

Yes.

Then, because of your awareness and the ability to understand that you don't like that commercial, does it give rise to your intention to change the channel?

Yes.

And so you do. In that simple moment, you experience your true self: awareness and intention or energy. Everything allows you to experience your power of intention as you interact with it. Because you can collaborate with your body, and your body has a finger, you can witness – though your awareness - your power of intention as you intend to move it and it wiggles. If there was nothing to interact with, how could you ever experience your ability to do so? And, while the things we interact with allow us to experience ourselves, they're still not who we are and thus completely identifying with them makes little sense.

Letting go makes much more sense now.

I'm glad it does. Letting go is far easier when we understand that what we're letting go of isn't truly ours to begin with. Everything in your awareness is coming and going. It's giving you the ability to know and express yourself. Without it, you could not know the essence of your existence. You'd be space without walls or the kid without a different set of clothes and interests. However, latching onto those things limits you to that one false sense of what or who you are. If you latch onto fear or sadness, you are essentially saying, "I am this fear, I am this sadness." Not only have you falsely identified yourself, but you've limited your ability to experience your potential and the world around you by shutting off any other experiences that aren't fear or sadness. We're sabotaging our opportunity to truly know who we are, and knowing and experiencing ourselves brings us the greatest feeling of joy. No wonder, then, it causes us so much pain to identify ourselves with these passing things that are only trying to have their own experience.

Now, I feel bad for doing it. Can you tell me more about emotions? Since I'm just awareness, am I the one creating them or are they a result of the body and mind acting on their own?

Everything is made of energy. At the beginning of this conversation I stated that you're consciousness made of energy. This energy reacts to other energy. Energy vibrates. Higher vibrations translate in the body to emotions like excitement, anger, joy, and others that often initiate movement. What do you think lower vibrations translate into?

Sadness.

And others similar to it. Energy tends to vibrate higher when it connects with other energy. If you are limiting your experiences, you are limiting connection. If you limit connection, or experience a disconnection, your vibration lowers and you feel...

Sad.

So the short answer is: Yes, your essence creates the vibration that translates in your body as emotion. But remember, EVERYTHING is energy, or consciousness, and driven to have experience through connection and expression just as you are. That's why I stated that the things passing through you are trying to have their own experience as well. Once you initiate that energy, it's on a mission of it's own.

Can you explain further?

Everything, including your body and mind, is made of energy. If you block any of its functions, such as emotions, from passing though and having their own experience, they get stuck. You block it by holding onto to it and claiming it as your identity. It doesn't want to be identified as you, it wants to continue its own journey. It's got places to go and things to experience. It rises to dance with you and then wants to move on. If you keep holding onto to your dance partner, she's going to get frustrated, irate, and do her best to get away. Imagine yourself tightly grabbing her and saying, "I'm YOU now. You're my identity." How strange would that be in the human world? Would you ever do that? Of course not. So, let her go. Enjoy the dance, remember who you are, and be grateful that you were given a chance to dance at all. It was her willingness to join you for a moment that gave you an opportunity to experience yourself and this beautiful thing we call "life". How amazing!

11
WHAT'S THE PURPOSE?

What's the purpose?

Of?

Anything, everything.

Its purpose is whatever you give it. If an obstacle is something you look at as a building block to help make you stronger, then that's its purpose. If you think it's a problem and only meant to cause you hardship, then that's its purpose.

Is that all? There's no ultimate purpose for existence?

Oh, that. To exist.

Could you elaborate?

The purpose of existence is to exist.

That seems rather obvious.

Doesn't it?

There's nothing more than that?

There's a lot more, but you wanted the ultimate purpose. I made it short and sweet for you.

Can you elaborate, please?

Sure thing. Existence means it has to have something to exist with. How can anything exist without having something that doesn't exist to reference? Thus the whole relative world is created. I can't say, "That is 'right'," without having a "left" to reference. So, in order to exist there must be something else, something to experience. But if all....do you follow me so far?

I think so. You're saying that in order for all of us to keep existing we need to have something to experience so we know that we even exist at all. It's the same concept as my true self. Is that right?

Yes. Now, the key is you also can't keep experiencing the same thing over and over again. Otherwise we are back to zero and everything evens out thus no further experience. There have to be new experiences. This is why there's evolution. The driving force behind everything is experience and thus creation of something new. Or, more precisely, the creation of a new form out of what was already there. Nothing entirely new is created, just new forms are shaped out of what already exists.

Why is nothing new created?

Science tells us that energy can neither be destroyed nor created, only transferred and transformed. If the point of everything is to exist, why would anything be allowed to be destroyed and thus never again exist?

Good point.

So, here we are: existence perpetuated by experience. Experience is thus perpetuated by connection and expression. Experience is outward from our presence because we want to expand and create new experiences so we can keep existing. So, we are driven by the desire to connect with others energy and express our own. The act of expressing our own energy opens the door to connect with other energy. Every time a connection happens, it fires off a new unique experience and perpetuates existence via evolution of that new experience. You are designed to experience. Hence the torment you feel when you try to avoid experiencing anything you are meant to. But, even then, you are still having an experience. In that moment you've chosen to experience pain. You can't escape your nature. That's like liquid water trying to escape being wet. Your nature is to experience through awareness and intention driven by the need for expression and connection. As a person of free will, you have the luxury of choosing what type of experience you want to have.

Do you mean I can choose to be happy all the time?

You can choose what type of experience you want to have when connecting with other energy. If you choose to fight with your experience, you've chosen pain. If you choose to embrace it, you've chosen peace. The choice is yours.

So there's no individual purpose then? I mean, no one is destined to be an actress or a school principal?

People are destined to experience. Some people, because of their particular frequency when they're created by various energies coming together, may resonate more easily with other similar energies. If expressing themselves via acting resonates with them, then I suppose one could say they've been destined to be an actress. However, destiny is a funny word that gets misinterpreted. Just because one is destined doesn't mean one is going to find that frequency or live life within it. As I stated earlier, you have the choice to pick your experience. Furthermore, your frequency can change as you evolve, just as life's frequencies can change. Maybe you were born resonating with the frequency of an actress, but you later evolve into vibrating at the frequency of a bus driver. No matter what you choose, ultimately, you will be fulfilling your true purpose which is to experience and thus create new forms so we can all continue to exist via evolution.

So this means someone's destiny might be to become a sanitation worker?

Perhaps.

That's horrible.

Why?

Who wants to be destined to work around raw sewage all day?

That's a judgment. It's those type of judgments that can keep someone from finding their frequency and enjoying it. The only reason working around sewage would be horrible is because you say it is, nothing more.

I would never want to do that.

That's a shame, because that's where your frequency is vibrating at.

Really?!

No. I have no idea where it's vibrating at. Only you can tell. I just wanted to see the expression on your face.

Funny.

The thing is, we create all kinds of labels for the

experiences we have. Thus, some of the experiences never get to fully integrate with our being. We label anger and sadness as "bad" and then spend a lifetime trying to avoid them. By doing that, we limit our own experience and existence. Do you remember in the beginning I mentioned a relative world and how we must have "left" to know "right"?

Yes.

Well, sadness and anger are merely reference points that allow us to experience the other side which are joy and compassion. It's because we've felt anger that we can know the feeling of compassion, otherwise everything would feel the same. If everything was cold, how would you know what hot felt like? And once you've experienced a hot day, doesn't a cold drink feel refreshing because of the contrast?

Yes.

So the hot helped you to know the cold, and vice versa. Yet, we label our experiences according to what we think they should be. We believe things should always feel happy so anything otherwise is bad. But it's all allowing us to exist, it's all necessary for us to have any kind of experience of life.

So I can do whatever I'd like because my only purpose in life is to experience it? There are no rules? I can slap a baby or rob a bank if I want to?

I never stated there are no rules. There is always the law of cause and effect and the actions you take will forever obey this law. You have the choice to experience your existence in anyway you'd like. I'm pretty sure if you slap a baby you'd end up in jail and at some point feel remorseful, if not the brutal end of someone's retaliation for attacking a child. That seems like a mighty painful way to experience your existence. But, to each their own. Choose as you like.

This whole time I thought I had to find my purpose.

You ARE your purpose.

It doesn't seem very mystical or as mysterious as people make it out to be.

Sorry to disappoint you. It's all about perspective.

How so?

Well, you say it's not very mystical. However, I find it extremely mystical and amazing. You are awareness or consciousness. You are ultimately formless energy with the power to experience, a power which you neither created nor earned; it was gifted to you by that which some call God or Source. Your energy is driven by the desire to express itself and connect with other energy, especially energy vibrating at a particular frequency that you cannot see, hear, taste, or touch, yet can still somehow magically sense. This interaction perpetuates an entire Universe and is the same action being performed by stars millions of light years away. Everywhere you look, you see this energy excited to express itself within the confines of the system it finds itself in. Leaves grow big and green. Trees grow tall and strong, spreading their roots as far as they possibly can. Humans create businesses, engage in sports, form relationships, and play at the park. It's all consciousness eager to experience the world and express itself in it's own unique way. It's so eager to do so, it stretches the confines of the system it's in, creating more unique expressions of itself through evolution. You have been gifted, by an unknown force, the power to choose which experience of energy you want to have. This energy is translated by your body and mind as emotions, thoughts, and sensations, all of which are their own energies seeking expression and connection. This entire Universe, including you, is a flowing mass of energy creating new forms of itself so it can experience Life and continue to exist. I don't know, to me, that's pretty mystical.

12
WHAT IS GOD?

What is God?

You are.

What?

You are God.

I'm God?

Well, not just you. But yes, you are God.

That doesn't seem right. What is God?

What isn't God?

That doesn't help.

Doesn't it?

I was hoping for a better description.

There really isn't one.

So everything is God?

Why wouldn't it be?

I thought God created everything.

Exactly.

Then how could everything be God if God is the one that created it? Isn't that different?

Only if you believe it is. Perspective, remember.

I feel like you're not answering my question.

Maybe it's not the answer you want to hear. But, maybe it's the answer you need to hear. Maybe I should be asking you the questions. Why wouldn't God be everything?

Because I always grew up with the idea that God was the creator of everything. That God was over there, something apart from us.

Doesn't that same belief system teach you that God is omnipresent?

Yes.

Then how could God be in everything but only be over there and not over here?

I suppose He couldn't.

Do you think perhaps your idea of God is keeping you from understanding a deeper meaning of God?

What do you mean?

Well, when we already have a set idea about something, that can keep us from being open to looking at it a different way. It seems like your current idea about God isn't serving you well, otherwise you wouldn't have asked, "What is God?", you'd already have an answer that satisfies you.

I guess, on one hand it seems right and on the other it doesn't. God seems grand, something far greater than we are and so it doesn't make sense to me that "I am God". But, at the same time, I feel like I'm missing something. I can't quite put my finger on it. I suppose you're right, I'm searching for something more...meaningful.

God is an interesting topic. Nobody knows what God truly is. All of the scriptures in every religion have an idea about what God is. People truly feel they know the answer, but if you break it down to why they feel that way it's based on what they learned from other people's points of view and how that idea makes them feel inside. They may even say, "I FEEL like it's the truth." So, if we're basing the truth about something on what's been stated for centuries and our feelings about it, it's perfectly feasible to accept the Pagans view of the Sun or the Egyptians view of the Underworld. It's a shame that such strong beliefs, based on nothing more than personal preference and information handed down to others, are the cause of such destruction. The questions stand, then: What is everyone fighting over and what are they all even trying to understand? There must be something human beings have sensed or witnessed for millennium that has caused the creation of religions, spirituality, science, and other avenues attempting to grasp this undeniable yet allusive reality.

Are you saying religions are wrong?

I'm saying religions are opinions. They feel like truth because people's belief in them is so extraordinary. The stories they share, and their view of what God is, slowly became engrained in society over many years. From birth, children learn about a certain belief system and thus it integrates with their very being, creating a deep feeling of comfort and certainty whenever the subject is addressed or debated. And that's all fine. It's human beings trying to understand their existence and purpose. They're not wrong for this, they're only expressing their version of the answer. If we take away our pension for disagreeing with everyone's opinion that isn't ours, we can see that ultimately we're all trying to describe the same thing. We're just using different words.

What are we trying to describe?

We're trying to describe and answer our two most intriguing and allusive questions: Where did we come from and what is our purpose? We addressed one of those questions already. When you ask, "What is God?", you're really asking, "Where did we come from?", "What's behind everything?", or "How did all of this get here?" God is just the label we give to the answer, even though the answer isn't complete. We label it "God" and walk away feeling slightly better because at least there's some sort of answer now, even if that answer is just a made up word.

A made up word?

Sure. The universe existed prior to verbal language which means whatever created it - the answer to where we came from - existed prior to having a name and only has a name because we gave it one. Yet, we fight over what the right name to call it is. What a shame.

That all makes sense. But, it still doesn't answer the question of "What is God?", or offer an explanation as to why you said I was God.

I'm laying the foundation. I gave you the easy answer but you wanted something with more flare so I need to set the scene before diving into it.

Oh. Ok.

When we take away this name, or our need to hold onto a particular name, we can talk more freely about what "God" truly is from our perspective. Since none of us were here at the time of creation, well, no energy in the form of human beings anyway, all we can do is use the information in front of us to determine what God could be. If we look around, we can see life. Wait. First, do you agree that we can't possibly know how this Universe was initially created since no person was there to witness it and take record of it?

I guess. Science seems to be getting close to discovering it though with the Big Bang theory.

Actually, some renowned scientists now believe that the Big Bang was not the beginning but merely a continuation. And, that the Universe seems to have no beginning or end. How's that for a paradox?

I didn't know that. Ok. In that case, I agree we have no idea what happened.

Great, then we can focus on what we're actually able to observe. As I was saying, if we look around we can see life. The term "life" refers to energy because everything is made of energy. It's everywhere, even in things that we label as inanimate objects such as metal rods or rocks. These things have life, or energy, vibrating inside of them. Beings we believe are "dead" - another word that gets misinterpreted - have life beaming within them in the form of elements, Carbon in particular. Life is everywhere. Everything is living in some way, shape, or form. Do you agree?

I can see that. Yes, I agree.

And this life seems to have a way of knowing how to balance itself out. The bees help to pollinate the flowers which also provide the bees with what they need to grow their colonies. Water forms rain which hydrates the trees. Trees give us oxygen which allows us to turn that into carbon dioxide to feed other trees. If something isn't thriving in an environment, it adapts or transforms back into fundamental energy to make way for something that will be able to thrive, thus helping that environment to flourish as well. This system seems to perpetuate itself. On top of that, we have the energy that is the foundation of everything. What perpetuates the energy? What tells an electron to circle around a nucleus?

I'm not sure.

And that is the answer that invented the word "God". Do you see how when we're mentioning God, or asking about what God is, we are merely using a word that describes this unbelievable force or guidance system perpetuating the life we can witness?

Ah, yes, I can see that!

We may never know what that exact force is, but we can witness it working every moment of every day. We can see that nature works in a complex fashion, even without a human brain; the type of brain that biologists believe is a necessity for complex thought and planning. Science tells us that an ant lacks this type of brain. Yet, ants are capable of communicating with each other regarding where the food is, where the path home is, if the queen is in trouble, as well as planning and building complex tunnels and having the foresight to store food for later use. What is directing the ants to do this if they're not capable of executive functioning skills such as planning and problem solving? Electrons lack a brain and yet they know to circle a nucleus until it's time to jump to another one. How do they know when it's time? What directs them to be attracted to this atom and not that one? Did you know that cells remember how many times their receptors have been used?

I didn't know that.

They remember, it's amazing! Then, if they've been used too many times by external sources, they communicate with the body to stop creating that particular chemical that's binding to that particular receptor. How incredible! Yet, what has taught it to do this and what guides it to continue? What animates it?

I have no idea.

WHAT IS GOD?

To use a popular term, "God"! God is the underlying force that does this. Whatever God truly is, God's function seems to be to animate and direct life. God's what gives energy its energy. It's what runs everything you see. Thus, God is omnipresent.

That makes sense. God has to be in everything because everything is powered and directed by a force we can't identify or, as well call it, "God".

Exactly. So when I say, "You are God," I'm saying that God is inside of you, that you are made of God. I'm calling you by what you're made of, like calling a wave in the ocean "water", instead of calling you by the form God has given you which is "human being".

What do you mean by "The form God has given me"?

Did you create yourself?

I suppose not.

Then your form was given to you by whatever created you. Remember when we spoke about existence and expression during the time you inquired about the purpose of everything?

Yes.

Well God, that underlying force animating and

directing life, must be part of that expression. Remember, existence is driven by unique experience and experience is driven by connection and expression. Thus, you are a unique result of God, over billions of years, expressing itself and connecting in order to create unique experiences and continue existing. You are very much the unique expression of God. Many different expressions that previously existed came together in one amazing moment, like a matchstick coming together with a matchbox to ignite a flame, and that created another unique expression: You!

Whoa.

You can say that again.

Whoa. Doesn't that make me part of God, not God?

Same thing, different phrasing. You're saying that you're the wave (Human) that's made of water (God). I'm saying that you're water (God) in the shape of a wave (Human).

I get what you're saying. It all makes a lot of sense. But, I still feel like saying that "I am God" is not quite right. It feels like I'm not giving God the credit He deserves or that I'm being really arrogant if I say that.

I can understand your position. It's not a popular thing to say, especially because some religions have taught people that God is greater than you could ever be therefore you're not worthy of calling yourself God. Those same religions say God's perfect, and everything he does is perfect, but you're not perfect so you can't be God. To that I only have one question: if everything God does is perfect, and God created you, then how could you not be perfect as well?

...Good question.

And an important one too because it automatically sets us up for failure and struggle. However, I think what they're trying to say is accurate, they're just using a different terminology that seems to insult us.

What are they really saying?

That God is the underlying force that powers and directs everything perfectly and that you are a product of that force, not the original one. They seem to be saying that you're the wave but can never be the water, which doesn't make a whole lot of sense. Perhaps they're trying to lead people down the path of humility and service by suggesting that they aren't grand in anyway and should therefore spend time serving God instead of looking down upon others. Humble service of others can lead to a fulfilling life. And, since God is in everything, we are always serving God even when we serve ourselves. Regretfully, I think some people take their religion's approach literally and develop a false sense of self; a sense that says they're not worthy of greatness.

That's a shame.

It is.

Ok. I still have one question though. If I'm God, or made of God, how come I can't perform miracles like God? How come I can't create a Universe at the snap of a finger or raise people from the dead?

Who says you can't?

Last time I checked I couldn't walk on water or turn it into wine?

You've never been on a boat?

I've been on a boat.

Are you not walking on water when you're walking on a boat?

Very funny. You know what I mean.

I'm afraid I don't. Do you not have doctors that bring people back to life? Do you not have ways of converting water into wine by adding grapes into the equation? Are you not able to create a whole community of people that network and communicate while creating amazingly complex computer systems that act as their own little universe? Are you not able to create life by procreation?

I don't create life, God does.

Exactly. That life, or new expression, wouldn't exist if you didn't procreate. You are God in human form, therefore you, God, creates life as a human does: via procreation.

I don't know what to say.

"Whoa" seems to be appropriate.

So, I'm God. Or, an expression of God.

Yes sir. Why do you think you can imagine something and then create it? Do you realize that your children's book was just a thought in your mind until you decided it needed to become a physical reality in everyone else's life? You then took steps to turn your invisible thought into something tangible. You may think these things take a long time, and that God would be able to perform them at the snap of a finger. However, if you consider the time span it takes you to create a computer or to think of a building design and then turn that into a skyscraper, it's less than the snap of a finger when looked at in the context of the history of the Universe.

I've never looked at it like that.

You've never had a reason to.

So I'm God. Or a part of God. I'm powered by God. I'm God personified. Wow. I don't know what else to say.

You're not boasting when you say it. If anything, you're praising God. Imagine how your father or mother would feel if you went around telling everyone that you're not a part of them. You'd basically be disowning them after they presumably took so much time to care for and nurture you. I'm not saying God is a person with feelings, but disowning the amazing force that is responsible for your creation, that is always actively inside every one of your cells allowing you to be here experiencing life, seems more arrogant than claiming your birthright.

I see your point. Wait. If God is in everyone of my cells directing it at all times, does that mean God is directing the cancer that kills us as well?

Interesting question. The short answer is: Yes. The long answer is more complicated.

I'd like to hear the long answer.

The long answer is that cancer is the effect of a cause. Cancer is not a punishment, it is a function of Life that helps to keep balance. You can't hit a baseball thrown at you and expect the ball to not move. There has to be an effect to every cause. It perpetuates the experience and ensures that existence continues. Cancer is the effect of various causes, most of which were created by human beings in their quest to experience new things. These causes created cancers that now effect life. That effect also perpetuates new experiences in the forms of compassion, kindness, and more conscious environmental and personal decisions that are leading the world back in the direction of balance. You can say that cancer is becoming an eventual cause of human beings finally taking better care of themselves and the world around them to ensure their existence.

You make cancer seem like a hero. My grandfather died because of cancer. I know many people who have lost someone they deeply loved because of cancer. It destroys lives and wreaks havoc on the body. People suffer miserably because of it. I hate cancer.

I'm not denying it does those things. However, God seeks to perpetuate experience via expression and connection. Maintaining some type of balance that allows the entire system to move forward is important. If beings are destroying themselves and everything around them then how can anything ever continue to exist? Human beings are stubborn. They don't budge until the situation is so threatening that it forces their survival instincts to take over. Cancer was regretfully the result of people not budging so Life was forced to create an effect to their cause; a situation so dire that it has sparked a global movement to find a cure thus pushing everything back towards the direction of balance. Cancer is vicious, but there is beauty that grows out of it. Please try to find the light amidst the darkness while continuing to work on finding balance with the life around you.

I will try. It makes sense, it's just a hard truth to swallow. I've always thought of God as only love and now it seems that God can be pain too. Why do they say, "God is Love," then?

It's hard to say because I don't know whom "they" is referring to. A lot of "theys" say God is love. To give a general answer, the act of being loving is often thought of as being accepting and open. Love is also perceived as giving, an outward expression. As we already talked about, experience is dependent on connection and expression. This could be construed as love. Also, everything is awareness based. You are aware of how you feel and what's going on around you, this allows you to interact with it and thus connect to it. Remember the cells and their receptors? They must be aware of what's going on in order to interact with the other cells and chemicals. Awareness, by nature, must open to everything so it can react to all that happens. It's accepting, like a loving mother you can tell anything to because you know she'll never judge you. This acceptance, or awareness, is also why God is sometimes referred to as "I Am". "I Am" refers to presence, being, awareness; there are no labels. If you were to introduce yourself without your name, what would you say? "I am." You'd be referring to your presence. Again, the act of just being there, or "I Am", can be construed as loving because it does not discriminate, it's simply there, open and receptive. So, all that we think of as God can be perceived as love. The individual expression, such as pain, can still feel "bad", but the energy underneath it, God, must be aware and expressive, which can be seen as open, accepting, and giving, or love.

Thank you for this clarification. It brings me hope and strangely makes me feel more confident in my ability to succeed in life.

Of course you'll succeed, you're Life itself! The question comes down to what you want to succeed at doing. Do you want to succeed at being unhappy and the person that can't do anything? Or do you want to succeed at being someone that can accomplish whatever they set their mind to? The choice is yours and you will always be successful at whichever you decide upon because you are God and God never fails. The power is in your hands. Which experience do you choose?

AFTER THOUGHTS

In reading through these chapters looking for misspelled words and missing commas, I was given the unique opportunity to witness my mental journey as it unfolded. What I've come to understand, and what I was wonderfully reminded of while editing this book, is that we create a lot of our suffering due to the stories we tell ourselves about what's happening. A common thread weaved these dialogues together: Let the stories go.

When dealing with things such as agoraphobia, panic attacks, and derealization, it's easy to label them as "horrible" and ourselves as "broken". It stems from the frustration of dealing with it and wanting the struggle to go away. But, like the tree with the crooked trunk, these things are only a set of unique expressions; they're neither good nor bad, they just exist. They become a problem when we label them as such, otherwise they're just a part of life at that moment.

For example, if you are unable to drive to the store today because you choose not to deal with the fear of doing so, then that's simply a moment in time. If you feel sad because of it, feel sad; that's ok too. The feelings shall pass. It's when we label agoraphobia as "horrible", say that, "Our life is over," because we didn't drive to the store, and call ourselves "weak" for being sad that we create unnecessary suffering and transform a simple moment into a painful illusion. This concept alone has helped me tremendously in finding my way through these past three years. As I remind myself to rest in my awareness of what's happening, even the stories flashing in my mind and my tendency to indulge in them, I find that courage and a sense of peace comes over me during the most trying of times.

Everyone has something they deal with that can be difficult. Your neighbor may not have anxiety, but he might be diabetic or have cancer. Anxiety or derealization does not make you broken, it makes you a unique human being with a specific set of characteristics. They do not define you, they allow you to define yourself. They give you the opportunity to know your inner spirit, the strength and openness you're born with. They allow you the chance to find inner peace by learning how to let go, showing you once and for all that attempting to control everything in life is futile. If you can open your heart to that which makes you "broken", you will finally realize how strong and complete you really are. Will you allow yourself that amazing opportunity? I truly hope so, because you are very much worth it.

Also by Shawn Elliot Russell:

BE STILL, LITTLE TREE, BE STILL
A CHILDREN'S BOOK ABOUT DEALING WITH FEAR

"After facing a frightful thundershower that shook him to his roots, a terrified little tree learns the secret to weathering his fears and the storms of life."

This beautiful hardcover 32 page book is printed on high quality 105 lb. paper. Each book comes with a special leaf made of seeded paper that you can plant with your family or friends. Once watered, wildflowers grow and bloom, increasing our "be-leaf" that the storms of life can help us to grow.

Available on Amazon & bestilltree.com
$12.95 - Hardcover
ISBN-13: 978-0997269000

Thank you for taking the time to read
DEAR ME, LET'S TALK

Please, be kind to each other.
You never know what kind of storm someone
may be going through in their life.

www.ingramcontent.com/pod-product-compliance
Lightning Source LLC
Chambersburg PA
CBHW031447040426
42444CB00007B/1012